A REAL ESTATE AGENT'
TO OFFERING
FREE
HOME STAGING
CONSULTATIONS
(or Advice)

Barbara Jennings, CSS/CRS

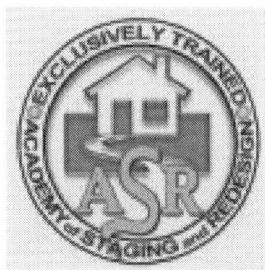

The Academy of Staging & Redesign
Decorate-Redecorate.Com

Copyright and Disclaimer

Table of Contents

Chapter 1
What is Home Staging?

What is Home Staging?

Home staging is the art of preparing a home for sale. The goal of staging is to successfully compete in the marketplace, attract more buyers, generate more bids and close a sale in the shortest amount of time. It has been well tested as a crucial strategy in marketing a home, especially in a tough market. As sellers must compete with a larger group of homes, whether they are distressed or not, they must be taught the importance of doing whatever is necessary to make their home stand out from the rest. In many cases, solutions are quick and simple. In other cases, solutions can be costly and time consuming.

Home staging is needed if:

- The home is in disrepair
- The home needs to be cleaned
- The curb appeal is negative
- The inside of the home is unappealing
- The home looks cluttered and uninviting
- The home is empty
- The furniture and accessories are poorly placed
- The home doesn't compare with other similarly sized homes in the area
- The home smells
- The home is dated and dull
- The home has been on the market for 2 or more months without selling
- The seller has had more than one agent

- The home has been taken off the market at least once
- The seller needs to sell as quickly as possible

Before I move into the full discussion of how you can learn to give quality staging advice to your sellers, let me first introduce myself to you and give you a bit of my background.

The Purpose of This Book

There are multiple purposes for writing this book. The first is to teach about the importance of the concept of home staging. While it has become increasingly popular and more widely accepted by agents and consumers alike, there is still a great need for education on the subject.

There is also some confusion as to the role of an agent and the role of a professional home stager which needs clarifying. Finally there is a need for agents to see and recognize the value of professional home stagers and how both sellers and agents can benefit from their highly specialized services. As sellers, their agents and stagers learn to work together for the benefit of everyone involved, the marketing of properties will become easier to achieve and profits will soar for everyone.

About the Author

I am a Southern California interior re-designer/home staging author and trainer and mentor to tens of thousands. My career in design began in 1972 when I started my own graphic arts and printing business. I staged my first home in 1975, only back then no one called it home staging. In 1983, having tired of the graphic arts business and seeing the handwriting on the wall with the invention of the home computer, I began a successful corporate art consulting career offering home decorating advice here and there for my corporate clients, and providing services in their homes that were separate from my art consulting services. During those years I designed and implemented hundreds of art collections for small, medium, and large businesses, including several Fortune 500 and Fortune 1000 companies. I also wrote and self published the popular book of 101 wall grouping designs called, <u>Where There's a Wall -- There's a Way</u> (now sold out but replaced by my book titled <u>Wall Groupings</u>!).

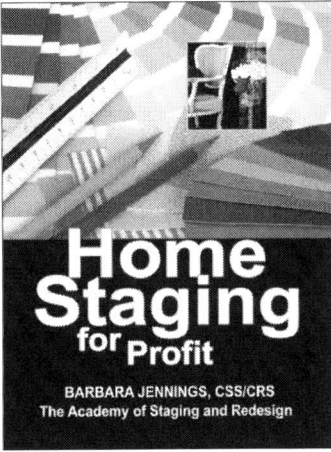

Since 1986, I have simultaneously served both corporate and residential clients with art and interior re-design and staging services. And in 2002 I began <u>Decorate-Redecorate.Com</u> and offered home study training in staging, redesign and art consulting for tens of thousands of eager entrepreneurs. These entrepreneurs have gone on to create highly successful businesses of their own. This manual has also been adopted by many colleges and universities as their premiere textbook for staging classes and certificates. Many who have taken my training and courses are also real estate agents. Almost all of them look to me as a personal mentor to help them grow their businesses or expand their services to their clients.

I have written over a dozen books and eBooks (which comprise basic and advanced courses), developed many professional sales and marketing aids, and pulled together highly effective tools to assist in the successful completion of staging and redesign projects.

In addition to that, I have become a published artist. My work has been published in the form of decorative art prints by The McGaw Group of New York and Galaxy of Graphics of New York, though they have sold out and are rare to find these days.

If you are interested in a course or additional training, visual aids and tools please refer to Chapter 26 for details.

Now that you know a bit about me, let's get to work to help your sellers make more profits and increase your commissions at the same time. The opportunity before you is endless. But you've got to have a firm goal in mind that is specific, and you've got to be willing to do whatever it takes to achieve your goals. If you have the passion, and you work hard, there is no reason why you cannot follow in the footsteps of those that have successfully gone before you.

Types of Staging Services

There are essentially two types of staging services:

1) **Consultation or Free Advice** – Simple consultation services (advice) is presently offered by many real estate agents as well as full service professional stagers. Consultation services merely amount to giving basic or detailed advice on what should be done by the seller. Sellers either do the work themselves or hire outside vendors to provide specific services. Consultation services offered by agents consist usually of advice only for simple cosmetic changes and is usually given to sellers as part of an agent's commission.

2) **Professional Services** – Full staging services that include both paid consultation and actual manual labor and other services are generally provided by professional home stagers whose business is devoted to the art of home

staging. Professional stagers offer a wide variety of services including (but not limited to): consultation and advice, landscaping, professional cleaning, light or complex repairs, renovation and upgrades, acquisition of additional furniture and accessories, furniture and accessory placement, enhancement tricks, painting services, window treatments and replacements, to name the most common. These services are fee based, usually determined by the size of the home and its needs to make the home competitive in the local market.

Real estate agents should not confuse the two services and should never offer "for profit services" for free. These more complex services are best handled by professional stagers who have taken in-depth training in the areas that pertain to a complex bundling of many services. Professional stagers usually are equipped to offer a wide variety of solutions to sellers in a cost effective manner. They will usually be able to accomplish the staging services quickly and professionally.

As a real estate agent, you will need to make an early decision in the best interest of the seller when it comes to staging services. Later in this manual I will identify specific questions you should ask yourself and questions for the seller which will help you determine whether the seller needs consultation only or the services of a professional stager.

As an ethical agent on behalf of the seller, personal profit should not be a factor. Maximizing the selling price potential and speedy completion of a sale should be the only concern. Many sellers will already be acquainted with home staging concepts and many will not. An ethical agent will work to help the seller by educating them on the full strategies available to them, and then assisting them in determining the best course of action for them.

Goals of Home Staging

While interior design concepts are heavily relied on in the process of staging a home for market, the goal is not to fully decorate the home as if someone were going to live in the home using those furnishings. The goal, instead, is to feature the structure (house) and make it feel as spacious as possible yet maximize its attractiveness and functionality at the same time. The goal is to provide potential buyers with a "move-in ready" property and assist buyers in fully appreciating the home's potential.

So the agent (and stager) should always seek cost effective or free ways of achieving the end goals. These processes are always in the best interest of the seller AND the buyer.

If a home is too decorated, too personal, buyers will have difficulty visualizing the home with their possessions. Buyers could also be distracted from focusing on the structure or be turned off by a seller's sense of style. For these reasons, the decorating of a staged property is kept to a minimum and color palettes are usually pretty neutral.

Some buyers have become suspicious of staged homes, feeling that somehow they might be tricked into buying the sizzle rather than the steak, so the speak. So it is important that sellers keep the property simple and straight forward and give the illusion that the seller still lives in the home even if they don't.

It is often said that a person should live in a home one way but should sell it in a different way. This is very true. Much of the time buyers would be turned off completely if they saw the home the way the seller really lived in it. This would not be fair to either party. But sellers should refrain from making the home look fully decorated and stylized and personalized. There is a happy medium – so when the agent, the seller and the stager all understand this, the results can be spectacular and exceedingly successful for all.

Why Sellers Need Help

After over two decades of staging and rearranging other people's furnishings and visiting homes where my services have not been sought, I have come to the conclusion that most people don't know that their furniture and accessory arrangements are poor. If they didn't know they had a need for a redesign service all the while they lived in the home, they can't possibly be expected to know now how to make the home attractive for other people.

If you don't know basic design concepts, you might not know that what you've done (or what you might advise) is ineffective. The most common problems I see are a failure to address a room's natural focal point, failure to create seating arrangements that encourage conversation, failure to balance a room, failure to create a sense of unity, flow and rhythm, huge disparities in sizes, failure to account for proportion and scale, failure to acquire a sufficient amount of accessories, failure to properly assess lighting and failure to maximize traffic lanes.

So what I find over and over again are homes that look and feel chaotic, choppy and totally unappealing. I personally wouldn't want to spend 5 minutes there, much less buy the home.

So while most people do a pretty good job of selecting reasonably nice furniture and accessories (to whatever point they have acquired these things), their sense of placement leaves much to be desired. Therefore their ability to make the home presentable to buyers will leave much to be desired. That's why there is such a need for home staging.

So this is one of the areas you may find to be the biggest challenge - convincing sellers that they have a need that you can dramatically resolve. Those agents who learn how to communicate the benefits of staging will have a marketing edge over those who don't.

What Sellers Need Most

The competition in this specialized service is growing every day. You are wise to add this service while you have a chance to dominate the market in your area. Sellers prefer to deal with agents that offer more than a basic service.

Home sellers need agents who are confident and really know what they're doing. They need agents who have a good head for details, are organized and methodical, know redesign techniques, understands the importance of repairing and cleaning - someone who can literally advise them how to enhance their home or who can lead them to a professional who can help them.

If there are specific areas of staging that you just prefer to avoid, do so. But consider building business relationships with a few professional stagers who would be happy to give you a referral fee to service your clients in those areas.

What will separate you from your competitors is your professionalism and service. Traditional design concepts, organizational skills, cleaning and repairing services and so forth have been around for decades. But the uniqueness of you, your ideas and creativity, your genuine warmth and commitment to service will be observable. Always be helpful. Good things will return to you.

But Does it Really Work?

Real estate professionals who use staging swear by it, no matter what part of the country they work in or the price range of the houses they list. The average real estate agent has five seconds to sell a home—five seconds to make an impact on the buyers when they first drive up to the home. Staging ensures that the impact is a good, lasting, positive one.

You can get staging ideas by looking at design magazines. Plus, you could go view several homes a week and learn what features interest buyers. You'll be able to figure out what doesn't work by your own reactions. Here are just a few examples.

One house listed previously was decked out in colors from the 1970s, with avocado green and heavy gold decor and a seller who didn't want to put much money into the house. The house had already languished on the market for three months, but when the home stager took over, the agent removed it from the market for a week so it could be prepared. She took out the old-looking lamps and furnishings and stowed them in the garage. Then she added subtle earth tone accessories in order to play down the greens and gold in the house. She removed the homeowner's artwork from the walls, replaced his outdated accessories with candleholders and plants, covered his shabby bedspread with one of her own and added mounds of pillows to create a cozy look. She even had her own gardener plant flowers for added curb appeal. The house sold in less than 30 days.

A sales associate with one major broker has been using professional stagers for about 10 years. "I believe that my homes sell quicker and for more money as a result of staging," he says.

He stages even his moderately priced listings. He recently hired a home stager to work on a condominium he listed at $184,900. The unit was vacant, and he knew that vacant homes are difficult to sell because buyers have trouble visualizing what they'll look like furnished. So he paid the stager $1,000 to furnish the bedroom, the baths, and the dining room, using props from her inventory. The result? The seller received multiple offers on the unit, and it sold within a week—for more than the listing price.

Some agents whose clients live in swank areas usually have impeccably decorated homes that need little styling. But when agents list a home, they rely on staging to give it lived-in appeal.

Another agent hired a stager to fill a 7,000-square-foot house with furniture, draperies, and accessories. Although he had not used the firm before, he was impressed that the company was able to stage the house within a week. The agent paid between $15,000 and $20,000 to stage the house, absorbing the expense himself and treating it as part of his marketing plan.

The payoff? The house, originally listed at $3.995 million and on the market for six months, sold within three weeks, for $3.75 million. "That house actually had very lovely architectural features but it was empty, and a lot of times buyers just don't have any vision. Once it's enhanced with furniture that is properly arranged, however, they can see themselves sitting by the fire."

Chapter 2
Free Advice vs.
Professional Services

Is There Room for Everyone?

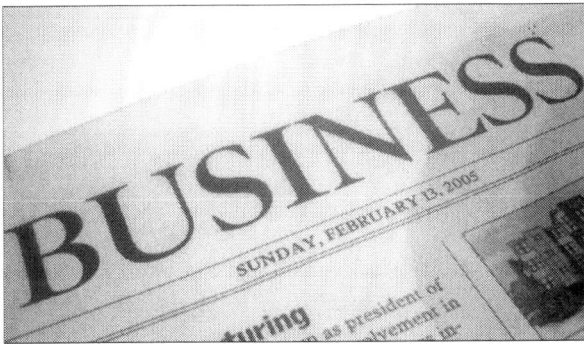

I've heard that some professional stagers question the idea of agents learning about home staging so they can advise their clients at no charge. At first glance, one can understand their feelings. They believe this potentially robs them of opportunities to profit as stagers. And perhaps it might from time to time.

But unless stagers contact sellers directly or are referred by an agent or other person, they will lose valuable opportunities. Professional stagers need agents to understand the process of staging and how important it is. Agents are on the front lines, so to speak, and are in the best position to help sellers understand the need for the service. And to that extent, stagers and agents are co-workers.

Each party relies on the other for help to do what is best for the seller so that everyone can profit. And stagers need to remember that a huge number of agents love what they do and recognize that their time and talent is better spent promoting their services as agents and not as stagers. This training is not meant to encourage agents to bypass stagers and do everything themselves. Quite the contrary.

It would be a major mistake for some agents to spend more than a cursory moment giving staging advice. But to whatever extent an agent gets involved, it is in everyone's best interest for the agent to have a measure of knowledge and talent so they are giving good advice.

It is each person's choice as to how involved they get in any particular service to a seller. Happily we all enjoy the freedom to conduct business as we see fit. Hopefully the needs and interests of the seller come first in all situations. But even there an agent must use his or her best judgment and that will always be subjective too.

It is important to be able to clearly separate in one's mind the difference between offering good complimentary advice (or as part of one's commission fee) and hiring a professional stager. Agents are asked to refrain from asking stagers to give free consultations or services. They deserve your respect. They have invested in specialized training, are professionals at what they do, and deserve to be paid just like inspectors or appraisers.

My suggestion to you is to gain the knowledge, which you are doing by reading this manual. Then search yourself and understand where your priorities need to be to maximize your personal potential for success. Focus your attention on what you do best. If you enjoy giving staging advice, by all means do so. Keep it simple. Get the seller to do all the work.

But have the good judgment to use professional stagers when there is a need for their more complex services. If you feel the potential is there for substantial profit, such as when staging a luxury home, consider paying the professional stager from your commissions if the seller is unwilling to do so. Just get it done.

There are enough houses out there with dire needs for staging advice and services. No one needs to feel their business will suffer because more people are educating themselves about staging. It should be good for everyone. As more people find out about staging and understand the benefits, there will be a lower need to spend so much time and effort educating the public. This will make it possible for stagers and agents alike to get the job done more efficiently and with fewer costs.

There is a revolving door out there for agents and stagers alike. You see, people don't go to college or university to learn how to sell houses or stage homes. They choose the industries for other reasons, such as the ability to work part time or to become independent. They choose to become agents and stagers because there is no limit to their income potential.

Just as there will always be people wanting to sell their homes, there will always be agents entering the field who know nothing about staging and there will always be people starting staging businesses. If everyone sees each other as a "team" member, it should be a good thing for all involved.

Chapter 3
Why Agents Should Offer Free Advice

Statistics on Staging a Home

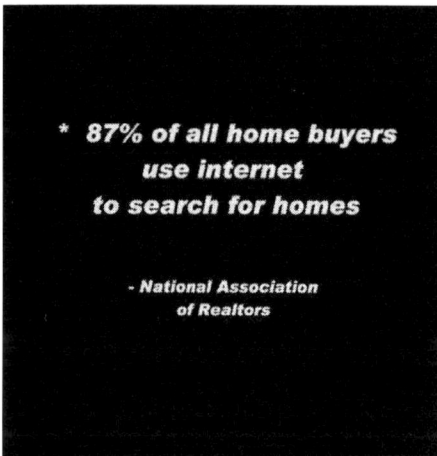

* 87% of all home buyers use internet to search for homes

- National Association of Realtors

Utilizing powerful statistics is an important strategy, not only to help you convince a seller that you are the right agent to sell their property, but statistics will help convince the seller that the home should be staged prior to putting it on the market. As an agent, it is your responsibility to make sure the home is priced right for the market, but also that it is competitively prepared for market. It should not matter whether you give free staging consultation as part of that objective, or whether a professional home stager is hired.

The goal is to get the home sold at the highest price in the shortest time frame. So it behooves all agents to spend the extra time and effort to make sure the home is ready for viewing. Statistics will help you convince the seller of the importance of staging their home.

Here then, are some powerful statistics that you should communicate to the seller in a verbal and visual manner.

- 87% of buyers use the internet to search for homes (National Association of Realtors)
- 63% of buyers will pay more for "move-in ready" homes (Maritz Study)
- A staged home, on average, sells for 17% more than an un-staged home (U.S. Department of Housing and Urban Development)
- Curb appeal ranks highest in all regions in value per dollar spent (Remodel and Realtor Magazine)
- 89% of sellers are willing to address recommendations by professional stagers (Real Estate Staging Association)
- 75% of sellers invest $500-$5000 in repairs and upgrades (Academy of Staging and Redesign)
- #1 factor in sale of a house is price. Other factors are condition, location terms, market conditions and home staging. (Barb Schwarz)
- Houses still on the market after 6 months drop in value by 10% on average.
- #1 factor in pushing price to a maximum for a quick sale is home staging.

Competition and Staying Competitive

Not long ago only about 6% of sellers used home staging as a strategy to get their homes sold. As home staging has become more widely known and as competition with foreclosed properties have made it harder to sell non-distressed homes, home staging has become even more crucial than ever. Instead of a handful of homes of similar size and location and price, now a seller may be forced to compete with hundreds or even thousands of homes. To make matters worse, buyers (who can qualify to purchase homes) are fewer and more savvy than in the past.

Smart agents are adding home staging consultation to their list of services like never before. To insist that home staging is not important is to provide a disservice to your seller. Home staging is more important than ever to both sellers and agents in this ever increasingly competitive market.

I have created a beautifully printed purse-sized Staging Statistics Portfolio booklet to show prospects and clients. They are incredible visual aids that you can easily carry with you at all times to help make the case for home staging, but to also present your specialized knowledge and talents as a agent. Visual aids are extremely helpful in driving that message home and helping you gain a pre-emptive strike over other agents who do not offer staging consultation and who do not know these statistics.

Benefits to Sellers

The benefits of home staging are varied for the seller, depending on the condition of the home and the competition they face. While no one can guarantee a higher price or a quicker sale, the average results are impressive. Each seller must evaluate the needs based on their individual property and their resources and their preparation schedule.

Obviously distressed sellers may be more reluctant to invest additional money into a property that is in jeopardy. They may not have the funds to do so at all. Your free staging consultation will be invaluable for them. There are many, many things a seller can do to improve the property that are free and easy to achieve. Simple furniture rearrangement, cleaning and de-cluttering can make a huge, positive difference.

One would think these types of resolutions would be common sense, but it is amazing how many people appear to be clueless. They think the house will sell just because it is put on the market. They may be disillusioned and depressed and don't care any more – or at least not very much. Their desperate situation may cause them to predetermine that the tasks are too overwhelming to accomplish and that time has run out.

Then there are the rest of the sellers. Some will just refuse to consider staging as an important part of their strategy or think that it is not up to them but up to you to work miracles.

But thank goodness there are still a huge number of sellers who will see and recognize the sensible benefits of investing some time, effort and money in strategies that will likely make them more money than they first realized. They just need someone like you to point out the benefits and the way to get there.

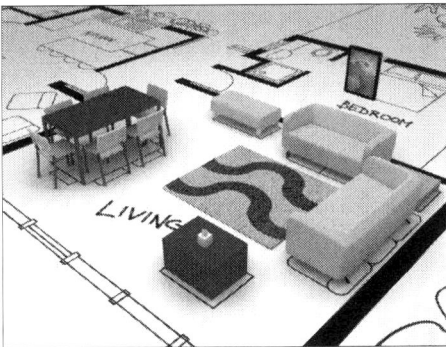

Our communities are full of homeowners who are ashamed of the way their homes look. They are ashamed to invite guests over. They are ashamed to put their home on the market but they have no choice. They know there are some major and minor problems with the home or the way it is decorated, but they don't know what to do about it. Their instincts tell them they have made mistakes but they don't know why their efforts have disappointed them.

That's because they have never been trained in home decorating concepts. They haven't a clue where to place their furniture. They don't know there are rules to be followed that make sense and that work. They don't know where and how to hang their pictures and artwork. They don't understand color and its importance. They are clueless when it comes to cleaning and repairing. They might live with mess in every room.

They could learn how to make their homes more attractive but they don't know where to get trained. Or they are just not motivated to learn. They would rather ignore the problem or expect someone else to fix things.

Never underestimate the power of pride of ownership. If you can show a seller how some minor improvements in furniture placement can make a world of difference, they get excited. They don't know how to solve the problem, but they sure recognize it when the problem gets solved. It is a light bulb moment for them. Instead of being complacent and ashamed of their home, they are suddenly excited to show off their home. They become motivated cooperative sellers when they see literal decorating miracles happen before their eyes.

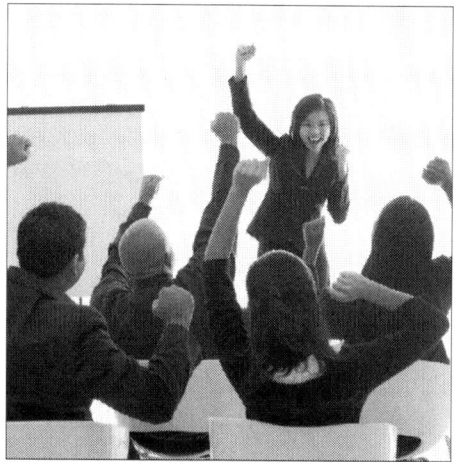

Helping a seller gain new insight into how a home should be decorated or arranged will benefit them long after the sale of the home is finalized. They will likely take their new found knowledge and use it in their next home. They will have this knowledge and skill forever and it will make a world of difference to them for the rest of their lives.

And assuming the staging has the average effect, they will most likely avert a price reduction (which would be a greater loss to them than the price of a professional home stager). They will increase their chances of receiving multiple offers that match or exceed the asking price. No one can guarantee this will happen, but it is a certainty it will probably not happen without staging the home properly.

Benefits to Agents

As more and more agents become knowledgeable about the benefits of offering home staging consultation and working with professional stagers, it will eventually become imperative for all agents to follow suit. We are not at that point yet, but every day more and more agents are adding staging consultation to their list of services.

It should also be obvious that if an agent offers a service that generates more bids on a property, the chances of the home selling for a higher price go up. Higher sale prices mean higher commissions. So there is a definite monetary advantage waiting for those agents who promote staging over those who do not.

As the public gains more knowledge about home staging, they will begin to expect staging consultation as an automatic service from their agent. They will demand advice because most people have trouble making the application to their own situation. They may have watched many staging shows on cable TV or newscasts or on various websites or YouTube, but they still feel they need someone to apply the concepts for them. They will look for affirmation of their own decisions and will always assume that you may have solutions they have not thought about.

As our global business environment is in a constant state of flux, it is the savvy agent who will continually stay abreast of what is happening that affects the market, both positively and negatively. You may be a bit hesitant at first to offer advice, but with time and experience you will get better at it. You may even opt to take more advanced training than this manual covers. See Chapter 26 for details on courses, books, visual aids and tools that are waiting for you should you decide to seek out more help.

Lastly, the staging strategies you learn will help you enjoy your own home more. These concepts and tactics work in any home and in any country. By applying them in your own home, you will marvel at their effectiveness. You may be able to transform your own home in a matter of hours. Your home will become more functional and at the same time it will be guaranteed to be more attractive. Your family will be amazed. Your own sense of pride in your home will increase and you'll find yourself eager to invite family, friends and clients over. Should you ever want to sell your own home, you'll know precisely what to do and how to do it. And should you need the services of a professional home stager, you'll know how to find a good one near you.

Important Principles of Staging

The purpose for decorating a family's home is to provide a comfortable, functional and attractive environment for the people who live there. However, as an agent servicing sellers, your job is to do all of that as sparingly and neutrally as possibly to appeal to the most buyers possible.

Comfort - In a day when most people work and are gone from their homes for the better part of the day, coming home should be a pleasant experience. They are tired. They may be irritable. They need to relax. So the more comfortable that experience is, the happier they will be. You need to convey comfort and relaxation to a buyer without all of the usual props and trappings found in a home where people are planning to live for a long time. You'll quickly discover that a home stager merely "suggests" an activity is possible. The stager doesn't necessarily go all out to provide what is needed, but just leaves enough to "suggest" an activity or feeling.

Function - The staged home needs to convey that the rooms are fully functional for the types of activities that are normally conducted in such a room. Typically one watches TV in the family room. The seating in that room should attempt to convey that activity. In the bedroom, the standard expected behavior is sleeping, so it makes sense to include a bed with plenty of room to navigate around it. Model home designers often place smaller beds in a room than would be normal. The bed suggests relaxation and sleep, but the smaller bed size makes the potential buyer feel that the room is quite large and easily navigated. It's not uncommon at all to find twin and full size beds in staged homes rather than king and queen sized beds.

Attraction - Making the rooms look attractive is a given. The seller must have access to furnishings on the premises (or rent them) that are compatible with the colors of the background of each room. If you're going to change the wall color or floor color, this needs to be determined after furnishings are selected for the room but before the furnishings are brought into the room. Attractiveness can be boiled down to two critical elements: color and placement. Get that right and the room will look terrific. Just think about a fine hotel room. It is designed to make you feel comfortable, relaxed and happy, but they only include the barest of furnishings and accessories. The rest is left to your imagination.

Chapter 4
Type of Sellers in the Market Place

Distressed Sellers

There will always be those sellers who are sitting on a time bomb – foreclosure. They are falling behind in their payments. Time is of the essence. They need help and they need it yesterday. Money is a critical issue for them. They frankly do not have the cash (or willingness) to hire a home stager. You'll be faced with giving them advice and hoping they can focus on doing whatever they can to spruce up the home and get it ready for market. Or you'll have to decide whether you feel it is worth it to you to invest part of your potential commission to help them.

Be very careful. I recently staged a home where the seller had already done several upgrades inside the home. It was a very low end property. I went to see if I could be of any help finishing up on what they started. To my dismay, the outside of the property looked pretty trashy. The roof was in bad need of repair. The driveway was covered in dried oil stains.

Brick work around the edge of the yard was in disrepair. The grass looked awful.

The front of the home looked so poor no one ever walked into the home to see the upgrades inside. It wasn't long before the house went into foreclosure and the seller lost everything.

Had the agent spent money on the property to help the seller out, he would have been out that as well. So be careful what you offer a seller when you already know their situation is dire.

Do It Yourselfers

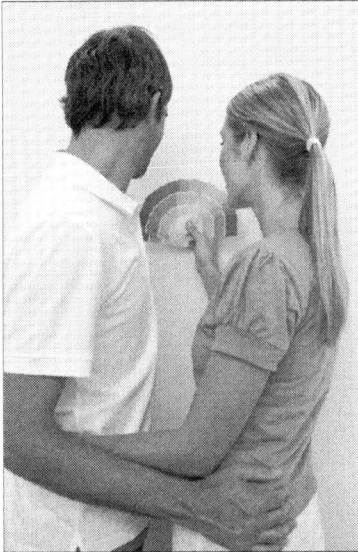

Don't expect that every seller will be interested in hiring a stager, no matter how affordable or advantageous it might be. Some people are just "do it yourself" people. I tend to be one of them, even though I fully recognize that there are many situations where I would be further ahead to pay someone. Let's face it. There are just some things I'd rather do myself, no matter how much time they take.

But for every person who wants to do it themselves or who just can't see past the cost of hiring a stager, there will be plenty of others who will see the value and not want to do what's necessary themselves. They will gladly pay someone to come in and handle the time-consuming details of staging a home.

So here is a nifty list of how to know, in advance, whether you're dealing with a do-it-yourselfer. You'll want to casually pose some of these questions to the seller directly.

- Do you enjoy doing physical work yourself?
- What is your level of patience and persistence?
- What are your work habits? Do you have good follow through habits?
- What is the time factor? Will you have adequate time to complete the tasks? (Note: The estimated time should always be doubled or tripled.)
- What kinds of tools do you have? Are they the kind of tools you'll need?
- What kind of expertise do you have in making repairs and other home improvements?
- What is your level of tolerating unfinished projects for a period of time?
- How much stress can you manage before it negatively impacts your family?
- How familiar are you with the necessary steps involved in each project?
- What manufacturer's instructions do you have on hand? Have you looked through them to understand the scope of the project?
- Will you need assistance to complete the job or can you manage it by yourself?
- Have you checked with your city for local building codes and permit requirements?
- Have you thought about what you would do if you are unable to complete the project?
- Is it safe for you to handle the project? What is the state of your health? (Some projects, such as fixing a roof, rewiring, and so forth are much better handled by professionals. One's health and safety should be priority ONE!)

Full Service Sellers

Fortunately there will always be a percentage of sellers who have the means to invest serious time and effort into the property in order to get the most they can get out of it. The older the home is, the more likely there will be a serious need for repairs, cleaning, de-cluttering, painting, upgrading, rearranging and so forth. These types of owners are prime candidates for full blown, professional staging services best delivered by professional home stagers – not agents.

Professional stagers are equipped to take on such projects and do fabulous work for the sellers at reasonable fees. They might charge by the hour or by the project. Some have been trained in seminars; some trained online, some trained in home study courses; some are self taught.

Due diligence should be made to narrow down the field and find the best person for the project. Not all stagers are equal. Some prefer to minimize their involvement to consultation only. Some use the services of rental companies when they need furniture and accessories. Some carry inventory themselves which they rent or loan to the agent or seller for as long as it is needed.

Some have been in the business a long time. Some are new start ups. Some profess to have designations from training companies. You should know that a designation is only as good as the trainer who issues it and not all designations are alike. Just because one designation is well known that does not guarantee that the person claiming the designation is good. Designations only have power because of the perceived value to the seller or general public. They guarantee nothing in and by themselves.

Some trainers do not give design training at all and some trainers, like me, feel design training is one of the most important ingredients in conducting a successful staging service. That is why you will be introduced to some basic design concepts in this manual. But you should know that you will only learn about some of the most commonly used design concepts – by no means all of them. In Chapter 26 of this manual you'll find access to in-depth design training to supplement what you learn here if you are interested.

Take great care when recommending a professional stager to a seller. Just as you will be taught to pull together a top notch staging portfolio to help you market your services as an agent, you should ask to see a stager's portfolio and look over the projects they have completed before making them part of your "team".

Trainers can create excellent materials for their students – but they have little to no control over how that training is translated into real world settings. There is no "one size fits all". Every home is different with its own unique set of challenges and must be approached with that in mind. The same can be said for professional stagers and re-designers.

Florida Home Staging and Interior Redesign Directory

Contact only if you are seeking the services of a member, otherwise please do not solicit them. Here are some of the top home staging and interior redesign specialists in the State of Florida. Each consultant is an independent entrepreneur and solely responsible for the claims and representations they make. Please locate the city near you for a professional in your area.

Home | Join Directory | Directory Home | List of States/Countries | Change Listing | Start a Business

City	Stager/Redesigner	Phone	Additional Info If Provided
Altamonte Spr...			...com
Altamonte Springs		40...	...com
Beverly Hills	Dee Raymond	(352) 527-8531 S/R	StagedRight4u
Boca Raton	Susan Stewart	(561) 477-7571 S/R	StewartRedesign
Boca Raton	Jill Greensberg	(561) 393-0657 (/)	twocheapchics@aol.com
Boca Raton	Joanne Lithgow	(561) 447-9230 (/)	jolithgow@aol.com
Boca Raton	Zuhal Cook	(561) 352-3471 S	zuhalcook@aol.com
Boynton Beach	Marilyn Geiger	(561) 364-5553 (/)	mwg1107@hotmail.com

In Chapter 25 you'll find links to my two directories where you'll find professional stagers and re-designers who have taken some or all of my training to help them become professionals. These are online directories hosted at my websites.

Chapter 5
Top Ten Most Common Mistakes of Sellers

Even under the best of circumstances, selling a home can be difficult - and most certainly time consuming. While you're not the seller, you should know the top mistakes that sellers tend to make. This will not only help you as an agent, but will help you help the seller and beat your competition in the process.

1. **As an Agent, You Must Know "Why" the Seller is Selling** – There's a difference between sellers selling because they "want" to and selling because they "need" to. The difference can color how the seller views the property and the stress they will feel. Sellers who just want to sell the property can take less aggressive means, list at a higher price and wait it out until they get what they want. Those that *need* to sell tend to be more aggressive and might even be desperate to sell the home in a hurry for a lower price.

2. **Under-preparation Before Putting Home on Market** - A seller won't get as much for the property

if they sell it in an "as is" condition. It will also take longer to sell unless it is properly staged. They tend not to keep it as clean as they should. Most buyers want a "plug and play" type home - one where all they have to do is move in. They don't want to have to repair and replace.

3. **Some Sellers Choose the Wrong Agent or Sell "By Owner"** - It's a myth to believe that because someone chooses to self-sell that they are saving money. All too often the house sits on the market for months, even years. It's important for them to pick an aggressive agent - one who is highly motivated to help them get the property sold. The longer a house sits on the market, the more wary potential buyers become, wondering from the outset what's wrong with the house. By marketing your staging advice, you'll show them you're not only aggressive, but extremely knowledgeable.

4. **Stale Listings** - That bears repeating. The longer a house sits on the market, the more wary potential buyers become. Even other agents start focusing on what's wrong with the property instead of what's right. If a house sits on the market for 3 months or longer, there is a significant problem that needs to be quickly rectified. If a home sits on the market for 6 months without offers, it needs to be pulled from the market, the price lowered or some significant work done to it by a professional stager.

5. **The Overpriced Home** - It's natural to want to sell a home for top dollar. But arriving at the correct figure will depend on several factors, not the least of which is condition, location and the current market. Failing to price a home correctly can be a costly mistake.

6. **Being in the Home During a Presentation** - Think about it. I hate to shop in stores where clerks follow me around, no matter how well meaning they might be. I'll walk out every time without buying anything. The same is true for selling a home.

Sometimes sellers hang around trying to influence a buyer's decisions. Unless they are acting as their own agent, this can kill a sale instantly.

7. **Showing a House That Smells** - The most common odor problems come from pets, cigarette smoke, strong foods and, yes, baby diapers. Homes should be thoroughly monitored by people who don't live there. Monitors will be more likely to pick up on a bad scent than people who live there daily.

8. **Failure to Make Final Mortgage Payment Before Closing** - Even if a contract has been signed by the buyer, it's vital that the home seller continues to make timely house payments on the mortgage. Most house payments are due on the first of the month. Final figures are calculated based on the number of payments the owner has actually made. Some get huge surprises, hit with late fees and have their credit dinged for failing to make that last payment on time. They don't realize that if there is any over payment, they will get refunded by the escrow company.

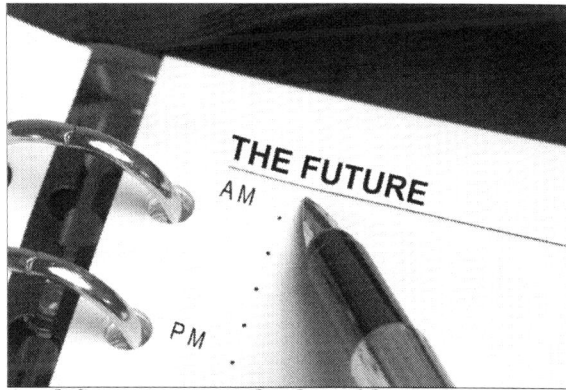

9. **Not Recognizing a Good Offer** - Typically the first offer a seller gets is the best one. But it's common for them to refuse the first offer, believing that a better one will follow. If the offer is close to the seller's minimum sales price, the owner should attempt to make the deal happen.

10. **Selling an Empty Home** – Buyers struggle with visualization. Yes, you can see the architecture when the home is empty, but it is much more difficult to

reach a buyer's emotions. Without connecting on an emotional level, the home is at a clear disadvantage when compared with homes that have furnishings.

11. **Setting a Poor Closing Date** - There are substantial tax savings for sellers who have lived in their home for twenty-four months or longer out of the last 5 years. Currently the IRS allows a single person $250,000 of tax free profit and a married couple $500,000 of tax free profit if they have lived in the home for 24 months or longer. If a home is closed in 23 months instead of 24, the seller will owe tax on all of the capital gains from the house, not just the excess over and above the figures stated above.

Don't assume that home sellers know these facts. A wise agent will use these typical mistakes to help sell their services and differentiate themselves from other agents.

Chapter 6
Top Ten Most Common Problems

Before you start talking to a seller about the cosmetic things you want them to do, it might behoove you to at least check into the top 10 most common problems that are universally identified as ranking high in occurrence.

1. **Structural Problems** - Obviously you're not likely to have expertise in this area. But at least try to look over the property with an eye open to this possibility. Structural problems can show up in the foundation, walls, the floor joists, the rafters, the windows and door headers. Look to see if there are any cracks in those areas.

2. **Environmental Problems** - Here is a brief list of some of the issues a home could have: radon gas, lead-based paint, contaminated drinking water, leaking underground oil tanks, asbestos, formaldehyde, carbon monoxide, pesticides. Many of these issues are not visible to the naked eye. You might want to ask the seller if any studies have been done on the property for structural and/or environmental problems.

3. **Drainage or Grading Problems** - If the property has improper drainage or grading, water can collect and lead to problems that produce mold. Look for damp basements or crawl spaces. The seller might need to have the exterior re-graded or have new roof gutters and downspouts installed. These types of things tend to be addressed by property inspectors, but it can't hurt you to be aware of these types of issues.

4. **Electrical Wiring That is Dangerous** - It's a common problem to find DIY sellers with improper electrical wiring. Many homes just don't have adequate outlets for today's lifestyle, especially since the home computer came along. Poorly installed electrical wiring can cause electrical fires putting every member of the family in serious danger.

5. **Poor Ventilation** - Look for damage to plaster, wallboard and windows which can cause poor ventilation. A home shouldn't be drafty, but it should also not be over-sealed. This can lead to rot and mold issues. Look for vents and fans in bathrooms with no windows. Check out the cooking areas as well.

6. **Roof Problems** - I don't recommend going up on the roof. It's dangerous and not your expertise anyway, but look from below to see if there are any obvious signs of roof damage, such as missing tiles or shingles, rotted wood, termite damage. Look for brown spots on the ceilings of the interior rooms, an indication of a possible leaky roof.

7. **Heating/Cooling Problems** - Look briefly at the water heater, and the heating/cooling units, usually placed in the garage. Blocked chimneys, leaking water heaters and the like are indications of neglect. Ask how often these systems have been serviced by a professional. Most of the time home owners ignore these systems until one day one of them stops working.

8. **Exterior Problems** - Look over the exterior windows, doors and walls where water and drafts can

enter the home. Whatever the seller can do to eliminate discomfort and lower the utility bills would benefit and bring about a better deal. Look for adequate caulking and weather-stripping.

9. **Poor Plumbing** - Look for annoying things like dripping faucets, leaky pipes and toilets, toilets that make noise when not in use, clogged drains. Plumbing is more likely to be a major problem in older homes where one can encounter leaky gas pipes, sprinkler systems that leak and so forth.

10. **Overall Poor Maintenance Signals** - It's not hard to spot poor maintenance issues such as peeling paint, jammed garbage disposals, rotting decks, light fixtures that are broken, or holes in the walls. If you see any of these types of problems it is a strong indication of much more to follow. There will, no doubt, be many things that you as an agent cannot and will not attempt to fix. But noting these things on your paperwork and having a brief discussion with the seller about their plans to correct these issues will only serve to present you in a more professional light.

Chapter 7
Identifying a Home's Faults

So let's say you have a seller with a house full of little negatives, nothing hugely serious, but lots of little problems that need correcting or, at the minimum, need to be de-emphasized. Recognize that buyers just seem to have a knack for noticing every piece of lint, every little smudge. They seem to make it their mission in life to find every little flaw. Don't be too hard on them. You and I would be exactly like them.

If a buyer sees clutter, they will invariably think the house is too small and not well maintained. They will be looking for other signs that support their impression - and chances are they will find the verification they seek. It won't matter one iota whether the impression is true or not. It's true for **them** and that ends the discussion.

Swimming pools may be a positive to some people and a huge negative to other people. High vaulted ceilings may be loved by one buyer but the next one only thinks about the expense of heating those huge rooms. The trick here is to make the house appeal to the greatest number of people while recognizing that it just isn't going to be loved by everyone no matter how great it is.

Some negatives the seller won't be able to do anything about. For instance, you can't go dig up the pool and dispose of it. But there are other areas where the seller can draw attention away from the negative "flaw" and push the buyer's attention in the direction you both want it to go. You just have to focus on the home's attributes while de-emphasizing the flaws. It only takes one person to purchase the home. You're just not going to know which person that will be. You won't know when he/she will show up. So to better your odds in finding him/her right away, you'll be advising the seller to put the house's "best foot" forward at all times.

Ask yourself (or have the seller ask themselves) this

question: *Does this room look brand new?* If the answer isn't "yes", then it needs work. You might not be able to make it look *as good as new*, but anything you do will help.

If a buyer drives up and sees weeds, peeling paint and such, they will immediately say to themselves, "This is a fixer-upper. I'll have to do a lot of work here. Not sure I'm interested or I'll definitely low-ball the offer." Some might even tell their agent to just keep driving. The seller is "dead" before getting a chance. And there are practically no second chances in selling a home. You either hit on the first preview or you're generally out of luck.

People buy primarily based on emotional responses. This explains why, when they fall in love with a house and can visualize living there, that the buying decision comes rapidly. The less work they see they have to invest to make the house fit their lifestyle, the quicker the sale and the higher the offer. Simple as that.

Chapter 8
Identifying a Home's Assets

On the other hand, your goal is to accentuate any possible natural assets the home has, and then even create the impression of other assets by the colors you use, the placement of furniture and accessories and the de-emphasis of the faults. Some of the assets you might want the seller to focus on might be things like:

- The phenomenal fireplace
- The view
- The flow of the rooms
- The large bay window
- The vintage bathtub
- The abundance of storage
- The cozy nook in the family room
- The two way fireplace
- The built-in entertainment center
- The security fence around the pool
- The spacious living room, great for large parties

Whatever you decide the dwelling's best assets are, these are the areas you especially want to accentuate. These are the areas which you will absolutely **NOT** compromise on as you give advice on how to enhance the house.

Have the Seller Seek to Portray Home's Potentials and Options

Not all assets are instantly recognizable. For instance, perhaps a bedroom can double as a den or office - or vice versa. Perhaps the family room could be converted into a library. Overly large rooms can be arranged to show two smaller rooms within the room, adding more flexibility. That recreation room could become an extra bedroom for a teenage son who likes loud music. You'll want to suggest ways to bring out a home's flexibility as well.

As I mentioned earlier, buyers will enter with a preconceived list of what they're looking for. But if your seller can show them more than one logical usage for a particular space, you might discover that becomes the sole reason they purchase the home, even if this aspect of the home wasn't on their list. Buyers will make sacrifices once in a while to get something else in return. But for them to sacrifice something on their list, like a home being closer to work or school, they must get something of equal or greater value in return. Your seller can help facilitate this alternative perceived value.

Chapter 9
Questions That Should Be Asked by All Involved

Rely on the insight you are able to gather as the agent, especially if you have been in the field for many years. You're likely to find it a give-and-take exchange with the seller. You will have certain types of information and data you need to give, as well as gather. You will have data and recommendations to make, as well as questions to be asked of yourself. Following are two such lists of questions you should ask yourself:

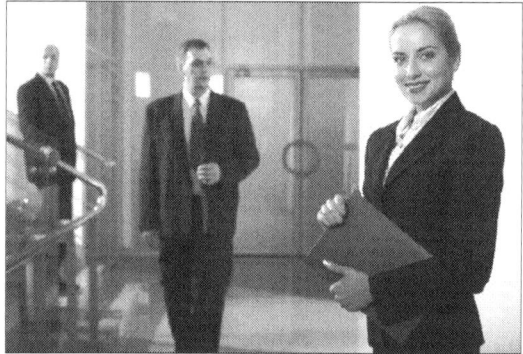

1. What are the time constraints of the seller – is time of the essence?
2. What are my own time constraints?
3. What are the financial circumstances of the seller?
4. Am I the first agent or have there been other agents before me?
5. If I am not the first agent, how long has the property been on the market overall (including past listings)?
6. Have there been any price reductions to date? How much?

7. What changes, if any, were made between listings?
8. What is the seller's sense of urgency?
9. Should I offer free advice or hire a professional stager?
10. If a professional stager is employed, who will pay for the services, when and how?
11. How much time do I think this property needs before it can be listed (or listed again)?

Write down your answers to the questions you pose to yourself. Not only will you be less apt to forget something important, you'll be viewed as someone who really cares what the other person is saying.

Questions a Stager Might Ask You

So let's briefly discuss some questions a professional stager might want to ask you. These are not in any ironclad order. You will find as you begin talking to a stager that the order will be affected by what each party is saying. You will probably think of information you wish to add to the mix, especially if something the stager says triggers an unusual request, suggestion or comment.

1. How long have you been an agent (broker)?
2. Have you ever heard of home staging before (home staging, staged homes, ready to sell services, etc.)?
3. If not, may I show you a brief presentation which will show you what it is and how it can benefit you?
4. Have you ever used a home stager/enhancer before on other properties?
5. What can you tell me about the property you have listed right now?
6. Are there any open house dates currently in place? When?
7. Has any company already inspected the property?
8. Are you the listing agent?
9. What can you tell me about the owners?

10. How long have they lived in the home?
11. How old is the home? What style is it?
12. Are they selling because they want to or because they need to?
13. Is the home currently on the market?
14. How long has it been on the market? If yes, are the sellers willing to take it off the market temporarily?
15. What can you tell me about any offers it has received?
16. What feedback have you received so far about the property from buyers, other agents?
17. Do you have pictures of the home?
18. Do you have measurements of the home?
19. Do you have a floor plan? Is it drawn to scale?
20. What kind of neighborhood is it in?
21. What is the asking price?
22. Are there any other terms that I should know about?
23. Will you be absorbing the cost of staging yourself or will I need to make a presentation to the seller?
24. What do you feel the major problems are in the home's current condition?
25. Are you interested solely in a Staging Plan or are you seeking a stager to handle all of the necessary tasks?
26. When can we preview the property?
27. Will the seller be present during the preview?
28. What price range do you have in mind for the services you feel are needed?
29. Do you feel the sellers are "do-it-yourself" types or will they want full service?
30. Have you already discussed a home staging service with the sellers?
31. What has been their reaction so far?
32. Is the home fully furnished, sparsely furnished or bare?
33. Do you anticipate the need for rental furniture?
34. How would you describe the general condition of the exterior?
35. How would you describe the general condition of the interior?

36. Will the sellers be moving into a new home locally or are they moving some distance away?
37. What can you tell me about the personalities of the sellers?
38. Are there any special deadlines I should be aware of?
39. What is the size of the family?
40. Do they have any pets? What kind and how many?
41. Is there a pool/Jacuzzi/sauna?
42. Where is the property?
43. How long have you known the sellers?
44. Are there any special personality issues I should know about in advance?

You will discover very quickly that a Q & A of this sort can move all over the place. You may be with a stager who has a huge amount of information to tell you and willing to do so, or you may discover the stager either has very little information or is tight-lipped. Some stagers will be open and friendly; others will be reserved and hesitant to share information. Obviously we'd all prefer the ones that are open, upfront, detailed and thoughtful. Don't be surprised if you're asking questions that they've never considered before or vice versa.

Chapter 10
Questions to Ask the Home Seller

Here are some specific questions you might consider asking a seller to help you understand your seller and the goals they have and to determine whether your home staging advice will be enough or whether a professional home staging service should be consulted. These are not the only questions you might ask but will, hopefully, serve as a starting point. Feel free to put them into any order that makes sense to you. Continue to ask questions and get feedback until you feel you comfortably have enough information to proceed. Depending on whether you're speaking to a "do it yourself" seller or someone open to advice and service, you may already know the answers to some of the questions and can drop them out of the list.

1. When you first purchased the home, what do you remember was the least beneficial part of the home that made you hesitant, if anything?
2. What sold you on purchasing the home originally?
3. After living here for some time, what negatives should I know about?
4. Do you know of any serious defects the home presently might have?
5. Do you plan to do any major repairs or improvements on the home yourself or hire outside labor to do them for you?
6. Has the home been inspected officially yet?

7. What has been the response of any agents that have previewed the home?
8. What has been the response of any potential buyers that have previewed the home?
9. Have you received any offers to date? What has been the disposition of those offers?

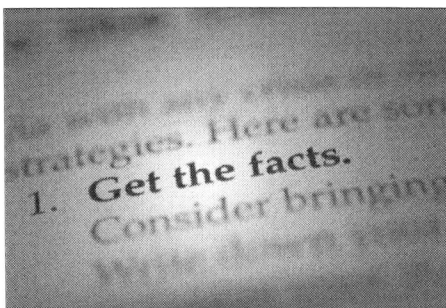

10. Have you already had one or more open house events? If so, what feedback did you get on the home?
11. Has this home been under contract with another agent previously?
12. Has this home ever been listed in the MLS or on social media? If so, what platforms?
13. What is the highest price this home has been offered at?
14. Have you taken any price reductions to date? How much? When?
15. What is your biggest frustration at this point?
16. When it comes to staging the home, are you looking just for consultation services from an agent or are you looking from someone to take charge and do all the necessary work for you?
17. Have you ever heard of home staging before?
18. If not, may I show you a brief presentation which will show you what it is and how it can benefit you?
19. Have you ever used a home stager before on other properties?
20. Have you previously staged a home yourself or received advice in staging?
21. I will need to take pictures and measurements of your home. Will that be ok?
22. Do you have a floor plan? Is it drawn to scale?
23. How have you enjoyed the neighborhood here?

24. Are there any problems with neighbors that I should know about?
25. Do you have any pets that get nervous when strangers are in the vicinity?
26. What do you feel the major problems are in the home's current condition?
27. Have you already removed any furnishings or accessories that are highly valuable or irreplaceable?
28. I may be suggesting the removal of up to 1/2-2/3rds of the furnishings presently here. Are you open to us moving them to a different location?
29. How would you describe the general condition of the exterior?
30. How would you describe the general condition of the interior?
31. Will you be moving into a new home locally or are you moving some distance away?
32. Is there a pool/Jacuzzi/sauna?
33. Do you plan to live here while the house is on the market?
34. Will you be living here until escrow closes?
35. If you are planning to move out before it goes on the market, will you be taking everything out of the home when you go?
36. Do you anticipate the need for renting furniture and accessories prior to putting the home on the market?
37. Do you have a budget for the services of a professional full service stager?
38. What is your budget?
39. $500 or less? $500-$1500? $1500-3000? $3000 or above?
40. Is there anything you can think of that would be helpful to me to know in advance?
41. Do you have any questions for me before we proceed further?
42. May we now take a tour of your home together?

You might say, "After I tour the home with you, I will need to tour it again on my own to take detailed notes, measurements and pictures. Is that ok with you?" Depending on the responses of the seller, you might not need to cover any more probing ground than what these questions have answered. But you'll probably find that the answers to these questions will generate other questions not covered here.

Questions can also be useful in confirming your understanding of what the seller wants, expects and needs from you. Those questions usually begin with, "Let me see if I understand you - is what you're saying . . . . .?" Or you rephrase or repeat something the client said and add the tag, "Does that sound right?" or "Did I understand you correctly?"

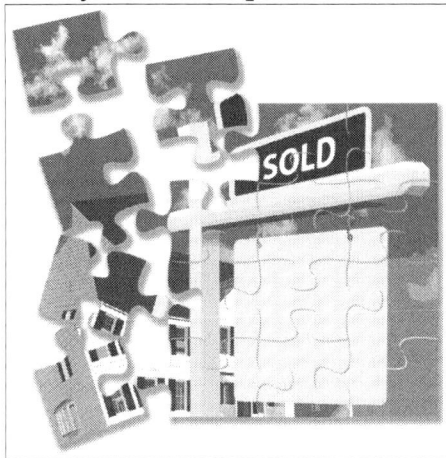

These types of questions help you clarify points and assure both of you that you are "on the same page".

During the interview process, your questions will probably be a mixture of different types of questions, but the majority of your questions should be open-ended questions, the kind that encourage the seller to talk.

The Give and Take Process

Regard the whole process as a "give-and-take" exchange. The person who asks the questions is the person in charge, not the one answering the questions. You want this time to be light and enjoyable for the seller and to create a feeling of having a conversation. Do not handle it in such a way that the seller feels they are being interrogated. So periodically, intersperse questions with information, comments and occasionally an example of what you've done for some other seller that may relate to the topic. Keep those examples to a minimum, however. If this is done very sparsely - a comment here, a similar experience there - the seller will get the impression you've had lots of experience, know what you're doing and have great confidence in you. If you are in the process of being evaluated against your competition, you should fare very well.

I was going to include an official form for you to use at the end of the book but decided against it as I think you should formulate your own with questions you feel are significant and in the order of your preference. So there is no "one size fits all" form I recommend you use other than one you create yourself. Forms can be very helpful to keep a conversation on target, but they can also limit the give-and-take process too. So for that reason, use them to establish a logical sequence for you but don't bind yourself to them.

Chapter 11
Touring the Home from Outside to Inside to Outside Again

The Initial Tour of the Home

When you start the first tour of the home with the seller, you're going to quickly find out that it moves smoothly and if the seller talks fast you can easily find yourself unable to write everything down that is being communicated. Don't be overly concerned because you're going to come back on your own (either now or on another day, assuming you get the listing) and take copious notes of every room or use the handy and thorough to-do booklets I've created for agents to streamline the whole process and give the seller the complete details of what needs to be done (see Chapter 27).

Your job right now is to listen, listen, listen. Your job is to ask questions as you see things that concern you. This is when you need to have your "buyer's eyes" wide open and take note again of anything and everything that bothers you now or bothered you on any previous tour you might have taken of the home. If it bothers you, it's going to bother other people as well. Write down the things that give you a poor first impression, which distract you from focusing on the house. Many of these impressions you will remember later, but some are really going to jump out at you and others you might tend to forget. Those are the ones you really need to write down. Pay attention to what grabs your attention at the end of the tour and upon leaving the home. Lasting impressions can sometimes be stronger than first impressions.

As human beings, we tend to remember forever the things that deeply affect us emotionally and we forget the things that didn't reach our deepest emotional levels. So that is why I want you to make notes about things you didn't like seeing that were more of a minor irritation, because these will be the ones that are harder to remember later.

Take a large note pad with you on the tour. Use at least one page per room. Note the name of the room at the top of the page. Jot down your negative reactions. Put major flaws on one side of the sheet and minor flaws on the other side. If you have time, note the positive reactions you have as well, as these can be emphasized later.

Taking the Seller's Tour

Keep the seller talking as much about the home as possible. Ask them to try to be brutally honest about any defects they know about as you would appreciate their help in pointing out things that buyer's might not appreciate or relate to. Make them part of the critical team. Praise them on their ability to separate their emotions connected with the home and their efforts to view it as a "house" and no longer as their "home". Make no value judgments. Make no comments unless you are asked specifically about something. Save everything for the end report you will be making using the to-do booklet I make available or one of your own making. Listen to what your seller is saying, but also listen for what they are **not** saying. Hopefully your seller will be totally honest about any problems in the home, but don't count on it.

If you are doing all of the talking, the seller isn't going to be very impressed. The seller wants to be heard and made to feel important and a part of the process. They may be apologetic for some portions of the house and its condition. Tell them you totally understand. Reassure them that minor defects can be easily fixed and that just a little tender loving care might be all that is needed. Be reassuring and positive. Be kind and understanding. Sometimes the homes will be in a state that is not normal for the family. You may not be privy to extenuating circumstances such as divorces, deaths in the family, some other critical issues such as loss of employment or other factors that can put a home into disarray. Be free of any judgment on their lifestyle.

Selling a home is a very stressful time for anyone. For some people it's like having a death in the family. I think about my own home of over 30 years and how I might feel if ever I was to move out. All of my family's history is in this home. It's undergone many changes through the years. It has aged with me and holds memories that are both near and dear and memories that are painful and joyous. There is a lot of history embedded into its walls that will remain long after I am gone. It isn't always squeaky clean. It isn't always orderly and organized. It certainly isn't in any kind of condition on the average day to be shown to a potential buyer. So you will **not** be privy to the deepest feelings, longings, or stresses of the seller. Whatever the condition you find, always show respect to the seller.

You're not likely to find a home that is in pristine condition. So the run of the mill will be homes that need help - some needing desperate help. It would be easy to fall victim to some kind of urge to be critical of the people themselves and not just of the condition of the home. Be on guard for that, especially if your own home is superior in quality or size to the homes you list.

Chapter 12
Making the Sellers Part of the Team

Creating Buyer's Eyes

Pricing seems to always be a concern of sellers (and with good reason). The wrong asking price can severely damage the prospects of a sale. And the wrong asking price can damage the amount of profit the seller will receive. But finalizing the appropriate asking price is outside the realm of this book. When sellers are eager to put the home on the market, they quite naturally are reluctant to spend more money to get it ready to sell, so here is where your specialized advice on staging will be of particular value and hopefully separate you from your competition. Sellers often don't realize that they are shooting themselves in the foot on price if they do not stage the home properly. They must be made to understand that either they need to stage the property themselves or an outside professional stager needs to be hired.

For this reason, you will need to educate your seller on the benefits and the necessity of staging the property. I have recently been involved in helping my business partner purchase property. We have been out looking for a couple of weeks so far, trying to narrow down the field and really determine just what he wants.

He has not found one house so far that has all of the features he wants. Maybe he'll have to settle for less, but he won't arrive at that decision until or unless he feels he has seen everything there is to see. I have been fascinated with the emotional and mental changes he has undergone.

In the end, while price is always an issue, there have been many positive homes we have visited and a host of negative ones. Of the 20+ properties we have previewed thus far, roughly half are empty and half are occupied. Only about 3-4 have been staged in any kind of appealing manner. Even when the agent knows about the concept of staging, staging has not been utilized, to the detriment of the seller.

I have the ability to see a home's potential and look past the clutter and badly chosen décor, but even I have been greatly affected by the cosmetics (or lack thereof) of a home. I can tell you for a fact that he nearly purchased a home that had been freshly renovated and beautifully staged, even though it was not exactly what he wanted.

A good night's sleep brought a more analytical evaluation come morning, but the beauty of the staged property was definitely alluring and very tempting. Had the features of the home been closer to what he wanted, an offer would definitely have been made.

Compare that to the homes that had more of the features he wanted but had red paint in the kitchen, or prison gray counter tops or broken steps leading to the front door. As a buyer, you really tend to focus on what's wrong, even though it might be something minor. Those things stick in the buyer's mind and they are hard to forget. I couldn't forget a giant smudge on one of the walls. Most people want a "move in ready" home, so the least little negative can register deeply in the minds and emotions of the buyer.

Going through a real life search for property with my partner has rejuvenated my focus so that I will be a better stager for my own clients. I recommend placing your seller in the same mode of a buyer from time to time. Take an afternoon with the seller and accompany them to some other homes of equal size and quality. Instruct them to pretend they are a buyer looking at these homes as a potential home for themselves. Not only will they see for themselves what their competition is offering, they will begin to understand the effects of faults and flaws and the need to see their own home with the same level of critical review.

Seeing Home as a Commodity

If the seller does not capture the need to separate their emotions from the home they have lived in and decorated according to their budget and taste, it will be very difficult (if not impossible) for them to accept criticism of the home. Failure to accept impartial criticism will keep them from having an open mind and keep them from making the adjustments that are recommended to them.

So it is vital, if you are their agent, to explain in advance that all critical comments are not a reflection on their personal choices or sense of style. Any criticisms will be mentioned because the home simply falls outside the scope of what the typical buyer might be looking for, based on data collected by agents all over the county.

Down the street from me a home went on the market about 8 months ago. The front yard is highly stylized with beautiful Japanese landscaping. Behind the tall cement wall is another Japanese garden featuring a koi pond and a deck. The koi pond extends into the back yard where it covers about ½ of the yard. There is another deck in back as well with a small grass area off to one side.

Inside the home, all of the windows are covered with shoji doors (simulated paper doors) so common in older traditional Japanese homes. The rest of the home has western design, but most of the furniture is Japanese style.

Even though the home (and especially the yards) is in very good condition, the mere fact that it is so highly stylized means it will appeal to a smaller number of buyers. Granted there are probably no other homes on the market quite like it, but it was not immune to taking a significant price reduction after it did not sell when first listed.

The agent either did not recommend removing much of the Japanese influence inside or was unsuccessful in getting the seller's cooperation. I believe this was a huge mistake. The home finally sold but not until a huge price reduction was applied, and even then it took another 4-5 months before it sold. I offered my staging services but to no avail.

If the sellers had been taught to look at the home with "buyer's eyes", they could have hopefully come to a place of removing some of the Japanese influence and making the home less personal. As it was, their family photographs hung everywhere, the furniture made the home feel less spacious than necessary, no attention to color flow or professional decorating had been applied and on and on. It was clear no staging advice had been given to the seller and no staging concepts had been used.

Gaining Seller's Cooperation

Unless a seller is open to hiring the services of a professional home stager (or unless you are open to that as well), you will have to rely on the seller to accept the suggestions you provide and to do so in a timely manner. Let's forget for a moment that everyone is busy – or so they say. There are going to be some sellers who are highly motivated, cooperative, energetic, and focused. There will be other sellers who are not motivated, not cooperative and not willing to work in an orderly, effective manner and against a deadline. The world is full of procrastinators. It is also full of those who will attempt ill-advised shortcuts to save time or to save money.

So you as the staging agent must keep tabs on the progress of any cleaning, repairing, removal, rearranging and so forth that you have recommended. For this reason, I suggest you have your seller sign a letter of commitment with you which outlines what they are agreeing to change in and about the home and specifies deadlines for them to keep (see Chapter 30). Failure to get them to commit to deadlines and do so in writing is just inviting failure.

People will tend to live up to the expectations you place on them but if you fail to place expectations, few will be self motivated to act on their own in a timely manner. There is something very powerful about signing a piece of paper.

People naturally take it more seriously. They also tend to believe it is non-negotiable. So if you have an open house event planned on a specified date, you've got to give them additional deadlines for achieving certain goals to get the home ready for a showing. If a seller is unwilling to sign such a document that holds them accountable for what they are supposed to do, then you should stress the importance of hiring a professional stager to do the work for them.

Commitment to the goals that are mutually agreed upon is vital to success. You'd be amazed at how many people will put off doing something they really don't want to do. As humans we are very creative in coming up with all sorts of legitimate sounding reasons for why we cannot do something. The reasons might really be legitimate too – but that doesn't change the fact that nothing is getting done and the home won't be ready to be listed or shown.

While signed agreements are not fool-proof, they will go a long way to making sure you and the seller are in agreement and they will help seal the importance of the staging tasks in the mind of the seller and the seller's family. See Chapter 30 for a sample commitment agreement.

Involving the Whole Family

Speaking of the seller's family, if the family will continue to live in the home during the time the home is on the market, it is vital to secure the cooperation of every member of the household – especially the children. As we all know, a home can look spectacular one day and look pretty cluttered and messy the next.

Take the extra time to get to know the family as a whole. Even greet the family pets and show appreciation toward them. Many people feel their pets ARE members of the family. Many an agent has been chosen as the listing agent because they befriended the family dog.

So when you discuss your written agreement and get the seller's signature as a commitment, allow the other family members to sign the agreement too. You might even factor in some kind of reward to younger children for successfully keeping their end of the agreement.

Believe me, when an occupied home is on the market, you need all the help you can get to keep the home looking pristine for the duration of the listing.

Gaining Commitment for the Duration

Getting the family to commit to staging the home themselves is one thing. Getting them to keep the home looking spic and span, organized, clean and in order for the duration of the selling process is altogether different. Since this is a common problem whether or not the home has been staged (either by the seller or by a professional), it is outside the realm of this discussion. All I will add is that you should plan for the worst, but hope for the best.

Periodically check with the seller to find out if the home is ready to be shown. Look for ways to keep them motivated. Compliment them on their continued efforts and remind them of how essential it is to a successful conclusion and the sale of their home.

Making Recommendations to the Seller

There are many different ways you can make recommendations, all equally good choices. Obviously, if you're just providing a consultation and you already know in advance that the seller plans to do all the work themselves, you can go through your checklist rather quickly and arrive at a to-do list for the seller. The checklist I provide is about as thorough as you'll find anywhere. Naturally there may be unique tasks for one home that are not necessary for other homes, so I have provided a place to record those. Because of this you can assure your seller that a checklist you provide will be customized for their specific home. Emphasize that your checklist is not generic in its entirety. You want the seller to know that you have given great thought and consideration to their specific circumstance.

Time is of the essence for you and often for the seller. So do not feel you should return to your office and generate a computerized list for the seller. It is not necessary and will waste valuable time. Recommendations are ideas, concepts and thoughts - as such they are more easily dismissed as being worthless or unnecessary if the seller doesn't understand them. I find it especially helpful to explain WHY a certain task is important. Once the seller understands the reasoning behind a suggestion they are far more likely to cooperate with making the change or adjustment.

In all cases, use good "bed side manners". Be gentle when making negative comments that require resolutions. Some people will have thin skin and will be apt to take criticism harshly while others will just be eager to do whatever you recommend. You should get a sense of your seller's ability to accept change during the interview process, but don't be too surprised if they become more emotional than expected when it gets right down to doing the work.

Men will probably not be as sensitive to criticisms about the home as women are. That's because women are the nesters and usually the ones who made the decorating decisions. But men often have a harder time with change in general. It is important to get the cooperation of both the husband and the wife to successfully move forward. You might even ask the question, "Which of you is the most likely to press on and get the job done, and which one of you tends to put things off?" Said in a humorous tone of voice, this type of question can let you know which spouse you will most rely on to get the staging done and done on time.

Chapter 13
Understanding Common
Home Styles

Evaluating Home's Architecture and View Points

It is important to begin every staging consultation with looking carefully at the home's architecture to see if there is any natural element in the home that should be emphasized. The same is true of each and every room or area of the home. You'll need to analyze the focal point to see if it is what you want to continue to feature and whether there is any aspect to it that needs to be repaired or cleaned up. This is crucial. Focal points attract the first attention of buyers and focal points give a room a central attraction from which everything else unfolds. They give a sense of hierarchy to the room and often reflect the main purpose of a room.

Some focal points are architectural and important to maintain. But there can always be situations in which there is more than one focal point or the natural focal point is not where the emphasis should go. In such cases, you may need the seller to create a different focal point to highlight.

For example, if the room has a large bay window but the scene outside the window is a neighbor's wall with their utility boxes, you're not going to want to feature that view at all. So draping the window might be in order, thus hiding the natural focal point. If the room has a fireplace but it is in some kind of disrepair and the seller balks at repairing it for some reason, you're going to need to draw attention away from the fireplace rather than featuring it prominently.

So you'll want to inspect the room's natural focal points carefully to see if they need service, highlighting or "hiding". Let's say that large bay window overlooks a grand floral pasture or beautiful woods but the window is covered with heavy drapes. You'll want to recommend removing the drapes (or tying them back) and hanging some beautiful sheer curtains instead where the scenery will open up and pull the buyer into the room to admire the view.

Nine Most Common Home Styles

Do you know your cape cods from your colonials? You can brush up on your residential architecture with this short discussion on home styles. It covers the most popular styles of homes in North America, including why some people prefer certain layouts.

Ranch - This style of house features one-level living. There may be a full or partial basement. Generally, a garage is attached to the side of the house.

These long, low houses rank among the most popular types in the country. The ranch, which developed from early homes in the West and Southwest, is one-story with a low pitched roof. The raised ranch (which is also common is the U.S.) has two levels, each accessible from the home's entry foyer, which features staircases to both upper and lower levels.

Split Level - This style of house became very popular following World War II because of the amount of space and utility provided. Split levels fall into two types: side-to-side and front-to-back.

This style of house is also referred to as a split ranch. The bi-level house is a modified version of the ranch house, with the major difference being that the lower level is more out of the ground than in the ground. Seldom is there a basement.

Split-level houses have one living level about half a floor above the other living level. When this type of home is built on three different levels, it is called a tri-level.

Colonial - This style of two-story house has been a mainstay of residential architecture for many years. These are generally well-built houses, with many being custom built. Their main appeal seems to be the spaciousness and elegance.

Dutch Colonial – the Dutch Colonial has two or two-and-one-half stories covered by a gambrel roof (having two slopes on each side, with the lower slope steeper than the upper, flatter slope) and eaves that flare outward. This style is traditionally made of brick or shingles.

New England Colonial – This two-and-one-half story early American style is box-like with a gable roof. The traditional material is narrow clapboard siding and a shingle roof. The small-pane, double-hung windows usually have working wood shutters.

Southern Colonial – this large, two-to-three-story house is world famous for its large front columns and wide porches.

Contemporary - These "casual" houses (see photo) are usually sheathed in redwood or stained hardwood and come in many sizes and shapes.

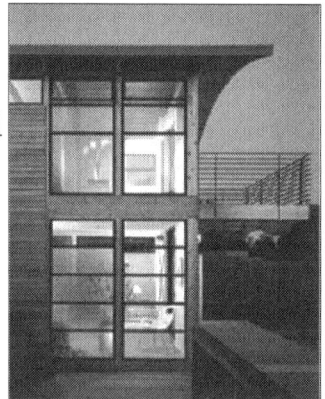

Cape Cod - This very practical one and one-half story style has been popular for many years, with most capes concentrated in the northern regions. Many resale capes have been expanded over the years for increased living area.

This compact story-and-a-half house is small and symmetrical with a central entrance and a gable roof. Brick, wood or aluminum siding are the materials most commonly seen.

Victorian - The Victorian style of house was built in various models during the turn of the last century. Home buyers appreciate the architectural nuances of Victorian houses including large porches and interesting bay windows.

Queen Anne/Victorian: Developed from styles originated in Great Britain, these homes are usually two-story frame with large rooms, high ceilings and porches along the front and sometimes sides of the house. Peaked roofs and ornamental wood trim, many times referred to as gingerbread, decorate these elaborate homes.

Townhouse - This style of house takes its name from the type of house which dominated the early residential development of our early cities, notably the row houses.

Tudor - Tudors and other English style houses were built during the period of the late 1800s through the 1920s. The combination of stucco and distinctive wood trim exterior provides the Tudor style house with a uniqueness which is most appealing.

Modeled after the English country cottage, Tudor styling features trademark dark-wood timbering set against light-colored stucco that highlights the top half of the house and frames the numerous windows. The bottom half of the house is often made of brick.

Pueblo/Santa Fe Style – Popular in the Southwest, these homes are either frame or adobe brick with a stucco exterior. The flat roof has protruding, rounded beams called vigas. One or two story, the homes feature covered/enclosed patios and an abundance of tile.

Georgian: Popular in New England, the Georgian has a very formal appearance with two or three stories and classic lines. Usually built of red brick, the rectangular house has thin columns alongside the entry, and multi-paned windows above the door and throughout the house. Two large chimneys on each end rise high above the roof.

Quickie List of 34 Home Styles

Learn about the home styles in your market and beyond. See if you can pick out your own home and those in your neighborhood.

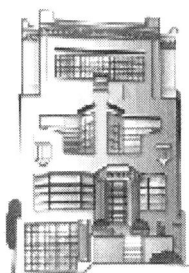

Art Deco

A vertically oriented design includes flat roofs and metal window casements.

Neoclassical

Neoclassical homes exist in incarnations from one-story cottages to multilevel manses.

Bungalow

A forerunner of the craftsman style, you'll find rustic exteriors and sheltered-feeling interiors.

Prairie

Originated by Frank Lloyd Wright, this style can be house boxy or low-slung.

Cape Cod

A true classic, Cape Cod homes have gabled roofs and unornamented fronts.

Pueblo

Flat roofs, straight-edge window frames, and earth-colored walls typify Pueblos.

Colonial

An offshoot of the Cape Cod style, it features a rectangular design and second-floor bedrooms.

Queen Anne

Emerging in the Victorian era, the style features inventive floor plans and decorative chimneys.

Contemporary

Unmistakably modern, this style has odd-sized windows and little ornamentation.

Ranch

Ranch homes are set apart by pitched-roof construction, built-in garages, and picture windows.

Craftsman

Full- or partial-width porches are framed by tapered columns and overhanging eaves.

Regency

The style borrows the Georgian's classic lines, yet eschews ornamentation.

Creole

A front wall recedes to form a first-story porch and a second-story balcony.

Saltbox

Its sharply sloping gable roof resembles old-time boxes used for storing salt.

Dutch Colonial

Colonial German settlers originated this style, which features a broad, barn-like roof.

Second Empire

This Victorian style features mansard roofs with dormer windows.

Federal

This style arose amid a renewed interest in Greek and Roman culture.

Shed

A subset of the Modern style, Shed houses are asymmetric with sloping roofs.

French Provincial

Balance and symmetry define the French Provincial style, which has a steep roof.

Shingle

An American style that echoes unornamented surfaces, natural colors, asymmetrical lines. The ever-present continuous roughhewn wood shingles on the roof and siding, feature cross gables, steeply pitched roof lines, and eaves on several levels. They have wide shade porches.

Georgian

With paired chimneys and a decorative crown, this style was named after English royalty.

Shotgun

Tradition says that a shotgun blast can trace a straight path from the front to back door.

Gothic Revival

English romanticism influenced this style, marked by Gothic windows and vaulted roofs.

Spanish Eclectic

This style has details from Moorish, Byzantine, Gothic, and Renaissance styles.

Greek Revival

Entryway columns and a front door surrounded by rectangular windows are characteristic.

Split Level

A Modern style, Split levels sequester living activities, such as sleeping and socializing.

International

The International style exposes functional building elements, including elevator shafts.

Stick

Decorative horizontal, vertical, or diagonal boards are typical of this Victorian style.

Italianate

This style has symmetrical bay windows in front, small chimneys, and tall windows.

Tudor

Tudors have half-timbering on bay windows and upper floors, and steep cross gables.

Monterey

The Monterey style updates the New England Colonial style with an Adobe brick exterior.

Victorian

Built during the rise of the machine age, Victorian architecture incorporated decorative details such as patterned shingles.

National

Rooted in Native American dwellings, the National style is rectangular with side-gabled roofs.

Knowing a bit about the style of the home of your seller, you can use terminology that is appropriate. Some minor research on the home style and traditional color schemes associated with the style would be recommended.

But bear in mind, your seller may or may not be concerned with the home's style. Many sellers purchased the home and brought in furnishings that have little or nothing to do with the style of the home. They may have brought in contemporary furnishings, yet the style of the home is Georgian. Or they may have brought in French Country or American Country furnishings, yet the home is a modern split level. The furnishings you find in the home will, in most cases, be the furnishings that will be used to stage the home, so don't be overly concerned with matching styles, or even color schemes for that matter. Neutral palettes still rule the day.

It is good to show an eclectic variety because one never knows what furnishings a potential buyer has or whether they are related to the style of the home or not. A good staging attitude should be to make the home look as spacious and as charming as it can look, regardless of style. So long as the colors blend, the furnishings are arranged attractively and functionally, and the home is clean, smells great and is in great condition, that's what matters with regard to staging it properly.

An eclectic mix of styles in the furniture and accessories will serve as relief to a potential buyer knowing how great the home can look whether their furnishings match the style of the home or not. Truth be known, I find it much more satisfying to find a mixture than a definite, precise style. It is usually more interesting to me and always opens up far more options as well.

Evaluating Background Design

After you've identified the focal point and decided upon featuring it or de-emphasizing it, then you'll want to turn your attention to the walls and the floor - the background of a room. Many people have chosen some pretty bright, busy wallpapers or dungeon dark paints and so forth that really make the home look small, dingy and foreboding. The carpeting may be in terrible shape and need replacing. The walls may need to be stripped of the wallpaper and re-papered or painted. The paint may be scuffed and marred or chipped. What we are willing to live with ourselves is not at all what we should suggest someone else accept - not if we want to sell quickly for top dollar.

Many people have chosen colors, intensities and values that are all wrong for the space. The walls and window treatments press in and attract too much attention. They don't blend in and stay in the background where they belong. Perhaps the seller has painted the walls dark and then installed bright white crown molding that just jumps out and grabs all the attention, making the room look choppy.

Your job as a staging agent should be to try to minimize some of the decorating faux pas and correct them by taking the background from glaring to subdued, from gaudy to neutral, from high contrast to a blended look. By doing this you will help the seller go a long, long way to making the entire home look more spacious and less cluttered. You will take it from poor design choices back into a safer, neutral zone that will appeal to the broadest possible range of potential buyers.

Evaluating Natural Light Sources

Next you're going to want to focus on the natural light sources of each room. Natural light is very important in making a room appear bright and cheery and welcoming. If a room has a lot of natural light, you won't have to make sure that artificial light is brought in, except for maybe one lamp for evening viewing. Let the light in as much as possible, unless it's the middle of August and the room is baking hot. Then you're going to want to do what you can to cool the room off during the hottest times of the day.

Natural light will also have an effect on the colors you recommend to the seller for the purpose of repainting. In hot climates, your recommendations should be toward cool colors; conversely, in cold climates you should consider recommending warm colors.

The direction a room's windows face can also play a part in determining color choices for the room. Rooms that get morning light will be affected differently than rooms that get afternoon light. One should note whether the windows face the north, the south, the east or the west. Rooms that have a lot of light throughout the day will be able to manage darker colors whereas rooms that get very little light should be painted with lighter colors.

Adding Artificial Light Sources

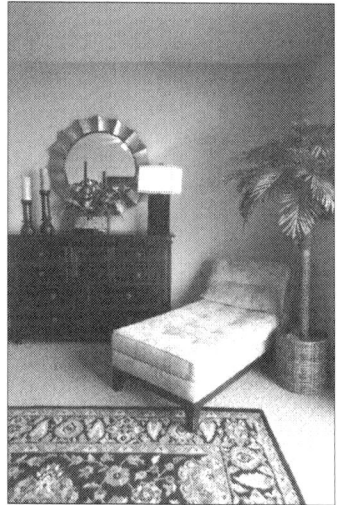

Whenever possible advise the seller to make sure there are at least 3 light sources that are positioned so that they form a giant triangle in the room. It's called triangular lighting. You want to light the room adequately, but you have to balance that with keeping the room from looking cluttered. Always remember you want each and every room to look as big and spacious as possible. So in some cases you may be faced with a trade off. More light vs. fewer items. Just use your best judgment here.

Lights should be left on when the sellers are not at home. It helps to brighten and make the home feel cheery and welcoming. In the evening, all lights outside and those on the front of the home should be left on until the sellers go to bed. It is common place for potential buyers to drive by a home in the evening to see what it looks like at night. Perhaps that is the only time of day they can preview the outside of a home or get a feeling for the neighborhood. The seller should work to make the outside of the home look fabulous and well lit whenever possible.

Bringing the Outdoors Inside

I'm a big, big fan of plants, both live and artificial. Plants are the easiest accessories to bring into a room and do absolute wonders for a home that needs staging. But the plants have to be in good condition. You can't have any half dead plants or plants with dead leaves. Instruct the seller to toss those babies out.

But as a staging agent you can keep a supply of plants on hand for just this purpose if you choose. You'll want to make sure that they are in excellent condition and marked on the bottom as being your property. Plants will soften the hard edges of a room and the furniture. Real plants will also introduce oxygen into the room and help the seller hide unsightly elements such as lamp cords, telephone jacks or electrical outlets. Plants are a seller's best friend. Having said that, don't overdo it. A little bit goes a long way.

Another reason I like plants so much is that they virtually go with any color and any style. You can use them with cool colors and warm colors. You can use them with modern furnishings and traditional furnishings and everything in between. Plants are also a type of accessory that many, many sellers don't have. All too often the plants they do have are very small and inconsequential or in poor condition. If you are recommending plants, tell the seller to buy or provide plants that have real substance – size. The plants can be taken with them when they move, so they are never an expense without ongoing value.

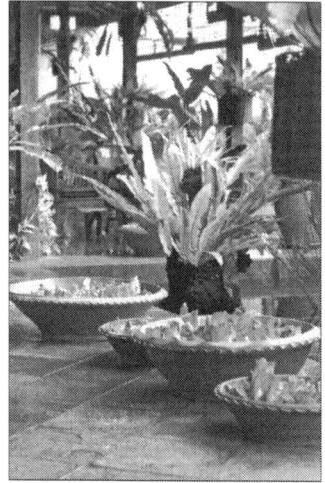

Chapter 14
Understanding Replacement Costs vs. Recoupment Possibilities

Return on Investment (ROI)

As of this writing you should find the following percentages pretty accurate, according to HomeSaleMaximizer.Com and their HomeGain Maximizer. In a nationwide study conducted by HomeGain, real estate agents identified 11 top home improvements that can add thousands of dollars to the sale of a home for minimal cost. Typical percentages range from a low of 94% to a high of 837% depending on the improvement and what part of the country the home is situated in. HomeGain has divided the US into four sections: Eastern, Western, Southern and Midwest.

Here is a list of the types of improvements they have tracked for more than a decade which can serve as a pretty good gauge in helping you advise the seller.

- Lighten and brighten
- Clean and de-clutter
- Landscape front/back yards
- Stage home for sale
- Repair electrical and plumbing
- Repair damaged flooring

- Update kitchen
- Update bathrooms
- Replace or shampoo carpeting
- Paint exterior walls
- Paint interior walls

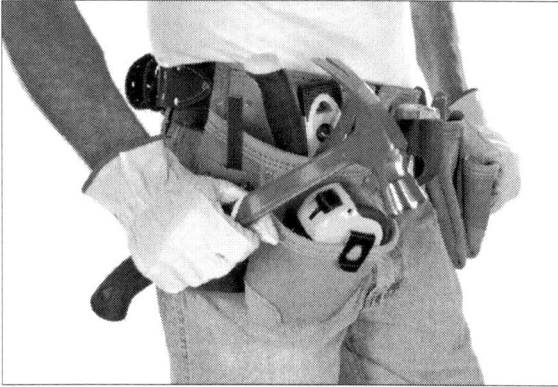

On the following pages you'll find worksheets I've prepared to help you assist the seller in determining the most valuable ways to maximize their budget. This is assuming the seller still lives on the property and will leave some furnishings to enhance the home. Obviously if the house is empty, more thought and consideration should be placed on renting furniture while the home remains on the market. A professional home stager should be hired to coordinate all of this.

Disclaimer: These figures were taken from HomeGain's current study and may have changed dramatically since then, either up or down. So do contact them at their website to get your own Maximizer that is as current as they have available. I present this information here simply to give you a reasonable idea but suggest you get the up-to-date figures directly from HomeGain.

Eastern ROI Worksheet

Lighten and brighten
TYPICAL COST	PRICE INCREASE	ROI
$250	$1700	600%

Clean and de-clutter
TYPICAL COST	PRICE INCREASE	ROI
$150	$2500	1567%

Landscape front/back yards
TYPICAL COST	PRICE INCREASE	ROI
$250	$1250	400%

Stage home for sale
TYPICAL COST	PRICE INCREASE	ROI
$350	$1750	400%

Repair electrical and plumbing
TYPICAL COST	PRICE INCREASE	ROI
$450	$1250	178%

Repair damaged flooring
TYPICAL COST	PRICE INCREASE	ROI
$625	$1750	180%

Update kitchen
TYPICAL COST	PRICE INCREASE	ROI
$1250	$3500	180%

Update bathrooms
TYPICAL COST	PRICE INCREASE	ROI
$875	$1750	100%

Replace or shampoo carpeting
TYPICAL COST	PRICE INCREASE	ROI
$450	$1750	289%

Paint exterior walls

TYPICAL COST	PRICE INCREASE	ROI
$875	$2500	186%

Paint interior walls

TYPICAL COST	PRICE INCREASE	ROI
$625	$2500	300%

Western ROI Worksheet

Lighten and brighten

TYPICAL COST	PRICE INCREASE	ROI
$250	$1250	400%

Clean and de-clutter

TYPICAL COST	PRICE INCREASE	ROI
$250	$1250	400%

Landscape front/back yards

TYPICAL COST	PRICE INCREASE	ROI
$450	$1750	289%

Stage home for sale

TYPICAL COST	PRICE INCREASE	ROI
$450	$2500	456%

Repair electrical and plumbing

TYPICAL COST	PRICE INCREASE	ROI
$450	$1250	178%

Repair damaged flooring

TYPICAL COST	PRICE INCREASE	ROI
$625	$1750	180%

Update kitchen

TYPICAL COST	PRICE INCREASE	ROI
$1250	$2500	100%

Update bathrooms

TYPICAL COST	PRICE INCREASE	ROI
$1250	$1750	40%

Replace or shampoo carpeting

TYPICAL COST	PRICE INCREASE	ROI
$625	$1250	100%

Paint exterior walls

TYPICAL COST	PRICE INCREASE	ROI
$1250	$1750	40%

Paint interior walls

TYPICAL COST	PRICE INCREASE	ROI
$875	$1700	100%

Southern ROI Worksheet

Lighten and brighten

TYPICAL COST	PRICE INCREASE	ROI
$150	$1250	733%

Clean and de-clutter

TYPICAL COST	PRICE INCREASE	ROI
$150	$2250	733%

Landscape front/back yards

TYPICAL COST	PRICE INCREASE	ROI
$250	$1250	400%

Stage home for sale

TYPICAL COST	PRICE INCREASE	ROI
$150	$1750	1067%

Repair electrical and plumbing

TYPICAL COST	PRICE INCREASE	ROI
$350	$1250	257%

Repair damaged flooring

TYPICAL COST	PRICE INCREASE	ROI
$875	$1750	100%

Update kitchen

TYPICAL COST	PRICE INCREASE	ROI
$1250	$2500	100%

Update bathrooms

TYPICAL COST	PRICE INCREASE	ROI
$875	$1750	100%

Replace or shampoo carpeting

TYPICAL COST	PRICE INCREASE	ROI
$625	$1250	100%

Paint exterior walls

TYPICAL COST	PRICE INCREASE	ROI
$875	$1750	100%

Paint interior walls

TYPICAL COST	PRICE INCREASE	ROI
$625	$1750	180%

Midwestern ROI Worksheet

Lighten and brighten

TYPICAL COST	PRICE INCREASE	ROI
$350	$1250	257%

Clean and de-clutter

TYPICAL COST	PRICE INCREASE	ROI
$150	$2500	733%

Landscape front/back yards

TYPICAL COST	PRICE INCREASE	ROI
$350	$1750	400%

Stage home for sale

TYPICAL COST	PRICE INCREASE	ROI
$450	$1750	289%

Repair electrical and plumbing

TYPICAL COST	PRICE INCREASE	ROI
$350	$1250	257%

Repair damaged flooring

TYPICAL COST	PRICE INCREASE	ROI
$825	$1250	43%

Update kitchen

TYPICAL COST	PRICE INCREASE	ROI
$1750	$2500	43%

Update bathrooms

TYPICAL COST	PRICE INCREASE	ROI
$875	$1750	100%

Replace or shampoo carpeting

TYPICAL COST	PRICE INCREASE	ROI
$625	$1250	100%

Paint exterior walls

TYPICAL COST	PRICE INCREASE	ROI
$875	$1750	100%

Paint interior walls

TYPICAL COST	PRICE INCREASE	ROI
$625	$1750	180%

Chapter 15
Understanding the Need for Curb Appeal

Creating Curb Appeal

While it is easier said than done, you've got to help your seller look at the home through the eyes of potential buyers. Anything and everything that enhances the outside of the home, particularly the front of the home, falls into the category of **curb appeal**. What did you first notice when you drove up to the home? Did you approach the home from more than one direction? If not, go out to your car and drive up to the home from as many different directions as possible. Only then will you see what a buyer will potentially see. My home can be approached from 3 different angles: left, right and straight on. Different aspects of my front yard are more noticeable from one direction than another. If I didn't look at every angle, I would not understand the importance of driving up from all three directions and inspecting the home each time from a different perspective.

The seller might have children who are popular in the neighborhood. Perhaps there are two bicycles lying on the lawn. The seller might find it necessary to do car repairs in the driveway to save money, but hasn't thought about the stains on the concrete left as a result. A buyer will look at these issues as junk in the yard and a home that hasn't been cared for very well.

Here are a few quick tips to pass on to the seller just in passing. Of course your advice will be more detailed after you have been contracted as the listing agent.

1. Keep the lawn mowed and watered and green
2. Keep the shrubs pruned and cleared
3. Store all tools, gadgets, toys, sports equipment, and other utilitarian items
4. Garage all cars or park them anywhere but in the driveway or in front of the house
5. Plant some flowers along the walk
6. Place some plants near the front door
7. Keep all windows sparkling clean
8. Keep doorbell in working order; install new doorknocker
9. Keep house numbers clearly visible at all times
10. Sweep sidewalks and steps daily and keep clear of clutter
11. Replace or repair walkways, stepping stones, fencing or bricks so they are in first class condition
12. Fix or replace all outdoor lighting; keep all lights on at night
13. Clean the new welcome mat daily

Creating Hearth Enhancement

The longer a potential buyer hangs out in the home, the better for the seller. If they are in and out quickly, you can be pretty sure they weren't impressed or it just didn't meet their needs. Since agents and buyers pre-qualify a home using some major criteria before even setting out to visit it, a quick preview is most likely caused by negative impressions the seller should have addressed but didn't. So it is the **hearth appeal** that will cause them to hang around, discuss how they would enjoy living in the home culminating in an offer of some kind.

So let's make sure we understand the criteria that buyer's most want from a home. If you don't understand what they want, you can't possibly try to give it to them.

1. They want a home that is spacious (or at least one that is clutter-free);
2. They want a clean home (they don't want to see bugs, pets, food, mildew, odors or junk lying around);
3. They want a home that is sturdy (free from squeaks, loose objects, broken objects or rusted and dirty objects).

Any home can be made to look spacious, even if it isn't. Believe me, the buyer already knows the square footage before arriving. But looking spacious is a feeling they get once they arrive. The seller could have a home with very large square footage, but if it is highly cluttered and messy, it will look much, much smaller and cramped. Counters that are bare can make a small kitchen look much larger.

Here again are some quick tips to pass on to the seller just off the cuff.

1. Get rid of anything that hasn't been worn or used in the last 2-3 years. Have a garage sale or donate it.
2. Remove excess furniture. Store it or sell it or donate it.
3. Clean out and organize all closets and cupboards and drawers.
4. Oven, dishwasher, microwave should be spotless.
5. Keep ceiling fans, light fixtures clean; replace all bulbs with new ones.
6. Tighten, repair or replace: hinges, switch plates, doorknobs, moldings, hardware.
7. Repair anything that leaks, squeaks, rattles or bangs.
8. Repair or replace anything worn, stained, smelly, frayed, broken, aged, or discolored.
9. Remove smudges, nicks, cracks, marks, chips.
10. Remove daily any trash, litter boxes, undone laundry.

Questions to Ask Yourself

Here are some very basic questions you should ask yourself when you are pretending to be a potential buyer the first time you ever set foot on the property. Set about answering these types of questions in a positive manner for the greatest number of people and you will be able to help your seller enjoy multiple offers. You will help yourself in the long run because multiple offers generally mean a higher selling price and, therefore, a higher commission.

1. What is there about this house that would appeal to me? To other buyers?
2. Can I easily entertain in a house like this? Would I want to?
3. Will my growing family fit in here? Or is this too much house for me?
4. Will this home be suitable for my particular lifestyle? For my business? For my hobbies?
5. How much work might I have to do to make it work for me?
6. How proud could I be of giving out this address to friends, relatives and others?
7. Can I live with any of the negatives I've seen?

Curb Appeal From Across the Street

I mentioned previously the importance of critiquing a home you want to list or have as a listing from across the street. It is even important to have the seller go across the street with you once you are the agent and making your recommendations. They will gain a perspective they have not considered and the feedback they give to you and to themselves will be invaluable.

Curb Appeal Within the Neighborhood

Don't just look at the home from across the street. Inspect the neighborhood as a whole and make sure that the home feels part of the neighborhood. If it sticks out like a sore thumb, you've got a major problem in curb appeal. I've never quite understood architects who move into a neighborhood and tear down a home and build a new home that is completely unsuitable for the neighborhood – just because they can't control their egos. I can't imagine the anger from the neighbors. And then there's the matter of its resale value.

Look for ways your seller can fit into the overall style and feeling of the neighborhood. Yes, individuality is great and important. But there are extremes that should be avoided.

Loud, outlandish colors that are not typical of the style of a home or the community should be avoided. If the house has a coat of paint that is totally unsuitable, you'll need to urge the seller to correct the problem. I'm not saying they need to switch to a bland, neutral palette, but it should be toned down. Cool colors on the exterior of a home are almost always the most appealing. Warm colors advance and may be overpowering.

Look at the flowers in the front yard or adjacent yards. See if you can find a subdued color or two that blend with the flowers in the yard already (unless choosing to fit a style). The color choices are many and varied but you don't want to paint the house a specific color only to find out all the flowers need to be ripped up and replaced because of color conflicts.

Color choices should also blend with the color of the roof. For instance, let's say the home has a rust tile roof. Well, one would not want to paint the walls pink in that case. Look at the color of the fireplace on the exterior. Does it need to be changed? For great ideas on coordinating colors for the exterior, I highly recommend a trip to your local hardware or paint store. Manufacturers always have sample brochures you can collect - some are even designed for the style of the homes in your part of the country that show color combinations you could suggest.

Be sure to tell the seller to buy small cans of paint and test the colors first before committing to any specific colors. When I was a novice I bought gallons of what I thought was the perfect black paint for the trim on a house. I did not test sufficiently. It was not until a great deal of the trim had been applied by the painting company that I realized my error. When the sun hit that side of the house, the paint color turned out to be a very dark blue, not black. Needless to say, new paint had to be purchased and the blue paint was turned into my primer.

Chapter 16
Understanding First, Last and Final Impressions

First Impressions

You only get one chance to make a first impression. I'm sure you've heard that expression before. In a relationship, the average time it takes to form a solid impression is 4 minutes. But when looking at a product, like a house, the time is shortened down to a few seconds - 15 to be exact. Buyers may not form sentences about their feelings right away, but their instincts are sharp and instantaneous.

Once a buyer forms an impression, they will tend to spend the rest of the time validating that impression as they move through the house. But if the first impression is poor, they won't give themselves a chance to validate it. They simply will move on without entering the home.

They will get first impressions about:

- The view of the house and neighborhood when they drive up
- The view of the front door as they approach

- What they see when standing in the entry
- An impression of the current occupants
- A strong impression in the kitchen
- Another strong impression in the bathrooms
- An impression when opening some closets and looking for storage options
- An impression looking at the yards
- And a final impression when departing

Each time they get a negative impression, your seller's fate is affected. They might overcome one negative impression, but it's doubtful they will be able to overcome three or more. Would you? Not likely.

Have you ever pulled into a gas station that was unkempt outside and in the food mart? Would you ever in a million years consider using the bathroom in such a place? Well, sometimes you're desperate. But normally you'd leave and go to a competing gas station or restaurant that is noticeably clean. Right? Well, another famous quote says, "Cleanliness is next to Godliness". So it behooves the seller to present a house that is spic and span, white glove squeaky clean.

If the seller doesn't have the time to clean thoroughly and a professional home stager is not involved, insist that they hire a professional cleaning service to go through the entire house and clean it thoroughly. Their industrial strength cleaners can make a huge improvement.

Last Impressions

Finally, before you ever leave the home on your first visit, the last thing you should study is how each room appears to you and the home as a totality upon **exiting**. Remember that the last impression can be almost as important as the first impression. What your eye is drawn to as you leave the room, or as you finally leave the home itself will create the lasting impression. Think of it like judging "Dancing with the Stars" or "American Idol". The last lift, the final position the dancers take is the last impression the judges will get. That final "high C" or that last musical "run" to end the song will be the last thing that the judges will hear. It's pretty important to leave a great lasting impression.

So make sure when you're taking your "before" pictures that you grab pictures standing opposite the doorway you entered in every room. If that's the last view you will get, that is the last view the buyers will get too. You'll want to make sure that view is as positive as their first view upon entering the room.

Final Impressions

Once a buyer leaves a property, he or she has formed a pretty solid impression – hot, cold, warm or cool. The first and final impressions have been implanted in the buyers' memory bank – but while emotions and impressions may run deep, there is a funny thing about memory. People will never be able to accurately remember things as they **actually** were.

Negatives may get blown overboard or minimized. The home will definitely be remembered inaccurately. They will either remember it bigger than it is or smaller than it is. They will not be able to remember colors with any kind of accuracy. They may forget nuances of the floor plan. Their list of priorities may have begun to shift. Emotions start to kick in. There may be disagreements arise.

These are reasons why smart agents have brochures or flyers printed with the specs and photos about the house. If you are representing a buyer, it would make a great deal of sense to make sure you have a wide variety of photos of any home you are showing and be able to produce a fact sheet listing the buyer's reactions to each property. It seems foolish to me to expect a buyer to remember every important detail to every home. What they do remember will not be accurate.

When they've visited 3-20 properties their memory will start to blur rather quickly and they can easily become confused. Having a good visual and a fact sheet that lists one's impressions is crucial when final decisions start to be made. As the listing agent, if you take your seller on a tour of the competition to get them to see the importance of staging their property, you'll want to have plenty of pictures and notes on each property you visit. You can use these documents and photos as part of your portfolio to help other sellers (and buyers) see you are on top of the market in ways your competitors are not.

The Importance of Photo Records

A good photo record is just as important for the seller to make available to buyers as it is to you for your staging portfolio. People don't do an admirable job of listening, usually. But a good visual will implant itself in their memory much more effectively and act as solid proof of your talent, recommendations and selling skills.

Retaining One's Impressions

As the agent of a seller, however, it is incumbent upon you to make sure that all buyers are given a detailed pictorial account of their visit to the property. You'll be able to photograph the home and the rooms from the angle you choose – the ones that enhance the property the best.

How sad to lose a sale because the buyer just couldn't remember how much they loved the home when they were in it. Pictures tell far more than words. I was amazed at how many homes my partner and I looked at which had no flyer or visual at all for us to leave with. Fortunately I took along my trusted wide angle camera and took my own pictures. But how many buyers will do that?

In the end, first impressions and lasting impressions all get merged into **permanent impressions**. It is those permanent impressions that will determine the fate of your seller's house. By sending the buyers away with a flyer or brochure with your well constructed photos and a staged property that looks fabulous, you will be heads and tails beyond the average agent and that is worth gold.

Chapter 17
Understanding the
Essence of De-Cluttering

The Less is More Effect

The popular design mantra "Less is More" was never more true than in home staging. This is probably going to seem pretty extreme, but when you start to de-clutter the home for the market you are going to take it from "full" to just this side of "stark". Seriously. You want to remove all sense of clutter and you want to make each room look as big and spacious as possible, but by the same token you don't want the home to look completely lifeless. Homes that are empty do not sell quickly. It's too difficult for buyers to imagine themselves living in the home. So you have to "suggest" activities by the furnishings you place (or leave) there. A completely bare room (or home) subconsciously transmits the message that the owners **have to sell**, that they are on the verge of becoming desperate to sell. This is not a good message for for sellers to transfer to potential buyers. You always want your client's home to look "lived in" – just not messy or cluttered.

Check out the number of doors in each room. If the doors are a different color from the wall, advise the seller to paint them the same color as the wall or remove them and store in the garage. You really want all doors to disappear from view. Doors, especially if a different color, have a way of cluttering the room visually because they chop it up.

When I arrived at a client's home a couple of years ago, her living room/dining room combination had 7 doors in a dark chocolate brown. The walls were off-white. The rooms were narrow and long and she had lots of furnishings. When I left I instructed her to have a painter change out the color of her doors to the same color as the walls. She was ecstatic with how much better the rooms looked and felt afterwards. After painting, her doors were not competing with her furnishings for attention and both rooms looked far less cluttered and relaxed with this one simple inexpensive "fix".

Check List of Removal Items

In order to properly de-clutter a space you'll need to advise the seller to box up accessories and other non-decorative items located in each room. The seller can purchase boxes from a moving company or search for discarded boxes from local retailers. Either way, as they box things up they'll want to mark each box with a label that states which room the box came from. It's also a very good idea to fill out a contents form and tape the contents form to the outside of the box (see our forms chapter at end of the book). There's nothing more frustrating than to be looking for an item and unable to find it after it's packed away. A contents list can be a value-added bonus you can offer that your competition won't have.

Some of the items the seller will box up will go into the seller's storage. Other items may be designated for donation to charity or even given to you for future props. By encouraging your seller to donate items you will be helping other people who need inexpensive sources for household goods, even clothing, shoes and other items. Some professional stagers now offer a **garage sale management service**. Your seller may find boxing up items that will be sold through that venue to be of value, either before the house goes on market or even at a different location, such as official swap meet venues or at a relative's home. Why go to the expense of moving and paying for storage of items the seller doesn't use any longer?

Encourage the seller to constantly think "less is more" and let that be the mantra of the day. Home owners become attached to items that they should have let go of years ago, so you can also provide a needed service of helping them look at many of their possessions with more objective eyes. If the seller puts enough items into a well-managed garage sale, they might even pay for a substantial portion of hiring a professional staging service with the proceeds.

But a word of caution. A homeowner's possessions often have nostalgic emotions tied to them. They might have really significant emotional feelings that get aroused by the sight of certain possessions. Be thoughtful and concerned about the memories that other people cherish that are associated with their furnishings - and the home itself. You might not have much appreciation for Johnny's refrigerator mounted drawing from kindergarten, but the family may be very proud of it. That beat up old rocking chair in the family room may look awful to you, but it may have been a life long treasure of Grandma who just recently died. To be cautious, ask questions about furnishings that don't seem to fit in or that are detracting. Once you know their history, you'll be better prepared on how to discuss their temporary or permanent removal from the home.

As you begin the process for the seller, remind them that it's going to look worse for a while before it all starts to look better. Weeding out and sorting possessions is a time consuming cluttered process. Remind the seller that all this upfront work will actually make their final move so much easier and has to be done anyway. It will also have another benefit when they get to their new home because it will also make the unpacking process go so much more smoothly end the end.

Typical Things to Have the Seller Remove From the Home

- Excess sofas and chairs. You only need one sofa and one chair per sitting room.
- Small throw rugs.
- Excess end tables. You only need two.
- All bookshelves except one.
- All ottomans.
- Boxes, bins, cabinets (more commonly found with home based business owners).
- All lamps except one table and one floor, unless room is extra dark.
- All small appliances except perhaps toaster or microwave.
- All stacks of newspapers, bills, notes, magazines, etc.
- All magnets, notes, bulletin boards.
- All large beds. Put in smaller beds with only one nightstand.
- One table and chair is enough in master bedroom unless room is very large.
- Television and stand in bedroom.
- Bureaus and dressers, unless room is quite large.
- All things on bathroom counters that are utilitarian.
- All but one bath mat. All extra towels.

Check List of Items Often Retained

You can temporarily fill out a checklist of items you recommend the seller keep in the room or get from another place in the home and tape this list to the door of each room. Just remember to have the seller remove these lists later when the process is complete.

Items commonly kept are: sofa, loveseat, sofa chairs, end tables, coffee table, console table, very large area rugs, dining table, dining chairs, smaller beds, night stands, table lamps, large trees, some plants, centerpiece, headboards, chest of drawers, large artwork, microwave, toaster. See the forms section at the end of the manual for an actual form to use for this purpose.

Chapter 18
Understanding Color Recommendations

Two Color Keys

When it comes to staging a home, the safest approach is to take the home from where it is into a neutral color palette. The reason for this is that the colors will have the greatest likelihood of blending with the furnishings of the broadest number of buyers. While this may seem rather boring, it really isn't if handled correctly. Even in a neutral color palette there are ways of adding color and drama to any setting, thus giving the space that "WOW" effect.

The goal is to get potential buyers to say, "Wow! I love this!" We also must remember that the home must not **feel** staged. What do I mean by that? Well, if buyers feel a home has been artificially made to look like someone lives in it, they are apt to feel the home might be overpriced or that the seller is trying to trick them in some way. So a great stager will make the home look very inviting without making it look like House Beautiful (unless it is a luxury home). The staging should fit the caliber of the home.

It is important the look of the home be simplified; that it makes the home look spacious, that it encourages buyers to see the home's potential by repurposing rooms to trigger possibilities, and that it look, in the end, **lived in**.

In addition to this, the home must not look too personalized. Color can turn off a buyer. They just might hate the color or can see right away that it won't go with their furnishings. So by neutralizing the colors in the home, the seller will advance the goal of getting the home sold. We're not looking for a home just to get sold – we want multiple offers to get the best price. And by far and away, the best way to generate multiple offers is to create spaces that are beautiful, clean, de-cluttered, fully repaired, not in the extreme and attractive. It doesn't have to win any awards, however.

So now that brings me to the two Color Keys. All colors are divided into two color keys. *Color Key One* is for cool colors (those colors that include an extra amount of blue, that recede in your vision). Cool colors are especially effective decorating colors in hot climates or where you want to create an especially relaxed feeling, like in a bedroom. Then there is *Color Key Two*. This Color Key includes warm colors (those colors that have an extra amount of yellow, that tend to advance in your vision). These colors are especially effective in cold climates or where you want to create a feeling of warmth and coziness.

There are many colors on the extremes of each Color Key and there are many colors in between one Key and another Key. You'll easily be able to recognize the extreme colors in each Color Key but it will be harder to identify the ones with very little amounts of blue or yellow contained. The less a color includes either blue or yellow, the easier it is to put it in a "neutral zone" and the easier it is to use it with any color. This is important to know because typically all colors in Color Key One will blend with each other and all colors in Color Key Two will blend with each other. But if one tries to use colors from Key One with Key Two, they will potentially conflict with each other, which is disturbing to the eye.

Mixing Color Keys was a big fad in the 1960s when fashion came out with the "psychedelic colors". They were merely mixing all colors together regardless of whether they were warm or cool. It made for garish combinations and I was only two happy when this trend disappeared. Unfortunately it may be on the horizon again as I just saw jewelry in a high fashion department store combining the two Color Keys together. I thought the jewelry looked hideous.

When choosing new colors to add to a space, one must be careful to recommend colors that blend and that are right for the space depending on other colors already there that will remain. Otherwise there might be problems.

For instance, copper and gold tone finishes on furniture and fixtures will look best with warm colors. On the other hand, stainless steel and silver finishes will fare better with cool colors on furniture and fixtures.

Value and Saturation

Value is defined as the <u>relative lightness or darkness</u> of a color. It is an important tool for the stagers, in that it defines form and creates spatial illusions. Dark colors are said to be **shades** of the actual hue (color) while pastels are said to be **tints** of the actual hue.

Contrast of value separates objects in space, while **gradation** of value suggests mass and contour of a contiguous surface.

So what does this mean to you? Well, darker colors (shades) of a hue (color) usually have black or some other dark color added to the true color. This subdues the color but tends to add visual weight. So, for instance, one would not paint a ceiling a dark color (or a shade of its pure hue). This would make the ceiling appear closer and heavier and would make a room look and feel smaller. The seller's goal should be to make the room look larger and the ceiling higher, thus the ceiling color should always be lighter than the wall colors.

What about **contrast**? Well, have you seen homes in person or in magazines with stark white crown moldings and dark walls? All the attention goes to the crown moldings. These types of rooms are usually pulled together by amateurs who don't realize that the crown moldings are probably NOT where one should draw that much attention. Don't get me wrong. Crown moldings and wainscot are handsome details, but in stark contrast to the wall color, they will focus attention away from more important aspects and make a room look overly busy.

Gradation, however, is a softening of color changes and an attempt to blend parts of a room together for a more pleasing, unified appearance. The crown molding might be a slightly darker or lighter color than the wall, enough to be attractive, but not in such high contrast as to turn it into more of a problem than an asset.

Saturation refers to the pureness of a color. A fully saturated color is the truest version of that color. Primary colors (red, yellow and blue) are fully saturated colors. They have not been subdued into a shade or a tint. In their purest forms they are very bright and as such, for the purpose of staging, should be restricted to a few accessories to give a room some "punch" or "wow factor".

Neutral colors give you a beautiful array of choices for staging a home. By limiting the use of colors, the space will take on a sophisticated appearance and the furnishings and accessories will be emphasized. The seller could experiment with fibers and other textures to add some decorating flair that is interesting but understated. This will infuse the home with a peaceful and calm feeling.

There are wide choices under the category of neutrals. Here are the most common and a safe bet:

- Grays
- Blacks
- Whites
- Blues
- Muted Reds
- Browns
- Soft Yellows
- Subdued Greens

Color Coordination

Generally speaking sellers should not add more than four general colors (hues) to a room. To keep the home looking spacious with the best uninterrupted flow, advise sellers to stay with 2-4 colors maximum for their palette. It is essential that the color choices blend with any furniture already present that will stay through the selling process. If there is no furniture, then sellers should find furniture first and choose paint colors later to blend with furniture than the other way around.

Wall colors should be subdued and visually remain in the background where they belong. The ceiling should be lighter than the wall, in most cases white or off-white. A client had put dark wallpaper on 3 of the family room walls because they wanted the room to appear warm and cozy (there was no 4th wall). When I staged the room, I painted two out of the three walls white (the two walls were parallel to each other). The room instantly appeared to be 2 feet wider than before. It's amazing what effect wall colors can have on the overall spaciousness of a room – not that the size of the room changes at all, but the perception changes. And when staging to sell a home, perception is everything!

Unity and Flow

Have you ever walked into a seller's home to find every wall a different color? Or have you walked through a home to discover every room is a different color? That may be ok for a family living there indefinitely because it is their personal style, but it's no way to sell a house.

In design we talk about **unity** and **flow**. Unity refers to how cohesive and unified the feeling is in a room and flow refers to how that unity moves throughout the space, winding from one room to another. The more the colors change, the less flow there will be and this breaks up the feeling of being in the same home.

That doesn't mean that each room is colored exactly the same way. What it means is that each room uses the same color palette, but the percentages of one color in comparison to the other colors in the palette change from room to room. In other words, let's say the palette for the home is blue, white and tan.

You would advise your seller to paint the living room with 60% white, 30% tan and 10% blue. But then when the seller moves to the adjacent dining room, there might be a switch. Now perhaps 60% of the room is tan, 30% is white and 10% is blue. Moving to the master bedroom where ultimate calm and a relaxed atmosphere is desired, the switch is made again. This time 60% of the room is tan, 30% of the room is blue and 10% of the room is white, or something to that effect. Blue is increased for its calming effect.

Can you see how just changing the percentages of each color will bring variety and interest to the home as a whole without disrupting its unity and flow? Whether the percentages get changed or not, and whether the entire home is painted one color, it is imperative to standardize the color palette for the whole home. Do not let your seller put a home on the market that is a mixture of every color under the sun.

Chapter 19
Understanding Paint Recommendations

Color Key One and Two

I've already discussed the two Color Keys and how one Key is for cool colors and the other Key is for warm colors. But what I didn't mention before is that there is a warm and a cool version of every color. There are stark whites and there are warm whites (often referred to as off-white). There are cool blacks and there are warm blacks. There are cool blues and there are warm blues. There are cool reds and there are warm reds. And you can't always tell which is which by looking at the paint sample chips at your local paint store or your fan deck. And you won't always be able to tell from the walls, ceiling or flooring either.

Paint companies do a pretty good job of dividing the colors from warm to cool and displaying them that way in their racks at the store. But it can be common to find all yellow shades and tints on the warm side and all shades and tints of blue on the cool side. So you have to be careful.

For this reason, advise your seller to pull many possible paint swatches from the store rack and bring them all back to the house. Paint choices should always be made in the environment where they will reside. Colors will change depending on the natural lighting in the room and colors will change at different times of the day and during different weather conditions. They can also be affected by adjacent colors and light bulbs. In an effort to keep this as simple as I can, let me just categorically state that one must never advise a seller to buy specific colors of paint without testing them first in every room of the house.

Instruct the seller to narrow down the choices as best they can and buy small quantities of each color. Then they should paint each color on the wall in every room and check the colors at different times of the day before committing all out to the final choices. This is the best way to avoid making costly mistakes.

Using a Fan Deck and Testing Colors

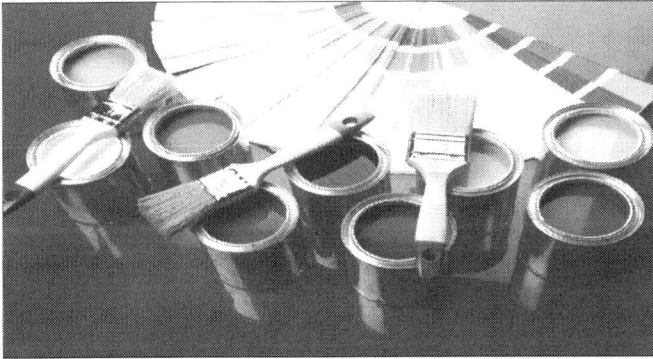

All paint companies provide fan decks to customers. You may need to buy one for your favorite brand and keep in your car. I'm not going to endorse any specific brand as you might not be able to get that brand where you live and I don't want to prejudice you one way or another. Check with several hardware or paint stores to determine the best quality and value for your sellers and go from there. If you tell the store that you will be giving advice to your sellers and directing them to their store for purchases, they might give you a fan deck for free. But at the most, your cost would only be around $15-$20 (or less) for a good one.

Visiting Your Local Paint Store

Encourage your seller to visit the hardware store or paint store and look at the displays of paint chips. Chips are always much too small in my opinion but that's not likely to change. At least they are working harder to make choices easier.

It used to be that you could have a color mixed and if it wasn't right bring it back for another one at no charge. Companies were using that as an incentive to sell paint. But I don't see those luxuries any more – now if you have it mixed, you've bought it. So sellers need to make the right choices on the front end to preserve capital and get the job done right.

The colors in the middle of the displays have the least amount of blue or yellow in them and can be more easily mixed with any color. The further the swatches are pulled from the outer edges of the display, the more important it becomes to stay on that side of the display for all the colors in the palette.

In other words, when selecting a paint color from the far right, choose other colors on the right side of the display to pair up with that color. If choosing colors on the far left, select other colors on the left to pair together. This way the seller will not run the risk of crossing Color Keys and ending up with colors that do not blend well with each other. That's about as simple and risk free as I can make it.

Chapter 20
Eight Most Basic Design Elements You Should Know and Implement

Here then are the most critical and useful rules of interior design as it relates to staging a home with simple advice.

Plan – Start with a plan. You never want to just start changing things without first developing a plan of action. Here is where the **Home Staging for Yourself** to-do booklets are so helpful. They literally are an instant customizable plan of action – a to-do list in bulleted format. The seller needs a plan on paper to serve as a guide over a complex process that will differ from house to house.

Proportion – Each room is commonly referred to as "negative" space. The furnishings in the rooms are considered "positive" space. The negative space is just as important as the positive space, even more so in staging than in redesign or interior design. The furnishings should be in good scale to the room, or undersized if you want the room to appear bigger.

When I was a corporate art consultant, we used different rules for determining the placement and size of art for a business. In a business environment extremely long walls must be divided visually into smaller segments that more reflect the size of a wall in a home. Then artwork is chosen to fit within the smaller segments. Seen as a whole, the art would be specifically arranged in vignettes or focal points along the corridor. The same rules for placement of art over a credenza and desk were applied as if the desk were in a home. But it was quite common for the rules of proportion to vary greatly in a corporate setting from a residential setting. So you could almost say that decorating for a corporate setting would be more closely associated with staging a home – less is more. However, a good rule of thumb is a ratio of 1:1.6 or roughly 2/3rds. Hang a 4-foot painting over a 6-foot sofa, for instance. Or hang a 2-foot painting on a 3-foot wall and so forth.

Scale – Scale is very closely aligned to proportion. But scale relates to the relative size of one element within a room as it compares to the other elements nearby. Scale also compares the width to the height of an element itself. Many times the terms scale and proportion are interchangeably used. Not to worry. The important thing is for you to know and understand the concepts involved.

Each element in a room must relate in size to the other elements – especially those in close proximity. It's important to avoid a <u>cliff-like</u> appearance from one element to another. For instance, if you had a large armoire in the room, you would not want to set a short chair next to it. The drop in height would be too extreme. The gradations in sizes should be gradual, creating more of a <u>rolling hills</u> effect. A very safe size reduction is by thirds. In other words, advise the seller to place a shorter tree next to the armoire. The tree should be approximately 2/3rd the height of the armoire, making for a gradual reduction in size that is not jarring to the eye. This rule also applies when making table arrangements.

When unusually small elements are positioned right next to tall elements and they, therefore, feel lost or dwarfed in comparison, they are said to be "out of scale" with each other.

The 2/3rds rule also appears when comparing the width of an element to its length. The Greeks figured out that the perfect rectangle is a 1:1.6 ratio (approximately 2:3 ratio). Have you ever wondered why stock frames for pictures come in specific sizes, such as: 3x5, 4x6, 5x7, 8x10 or 9x12? Even area rugs tend to come in these size increments. You can see how this ratio is used everywhere, not only for getting great proportions, but also for perfect scale as well.

When you're combining elements within a room, advise the seller to keep these ratios in mind. In fact it is so common place they will utilize this rule time and time again throughout the home. So get them used to thinking in terms of 2:3, 4:6, 5:7 and so on.

Unity and Flow -
Unifying a room (and also the entire home) is vitally important for best results. Color is a great unifying factor such as all black and white, all neutral colors, all primary colors and so forth. And repetition creates unity. Advise the seller to keep the same color palette in every room, adjusting which specific color dominates in each room. By changing the proportions of the colors in the palette from room to room, one can achieve variety and interest without destroying the unity and flow throughout the home. If contrasting colors are used together, it's important to spread them around the room to keep the room balanced. If you need to strengthen a particular color or tone, add other elements into the room that repeat that color, shade or tint.

Color – In my opinion, colors *must* repeat throughout a room and throughout a home. It is imperative that at least one color be repeated throughout the home for optimal effect. Good distribution of the various colors and values (shades and tints, brightness and dullness) should also be incorporated so it does not become monotonous.

Balance – Balance is a very important aspect of interior design and staging design and is the element which causes the most difficulty for many people. Here are some helpful hints in balancing a room:

1. Divide the room with imaginary lines down the middle, both horizontally and vertically. The left side of the room should feel equal in visual weight to the right side. The top should be well supported by the bottom, not the other way around. Look at the furnishings in front of a wall. Divide the wall in half vertically. Does the right side feel visually equal to the left side? Now divide it in the middle horizontally. Does the top half feel supported by the bottom half or does it feel top heavy?
2. Get a better feeling by blurring (squinting) your eyes. Do you tend to lean to the right or the left? If so, you probably have a balance issue. Adjust the right or left so that both sides *feel equal* in visual weight and your furnishings should be in balance.
3. Look at the room from several perspectives. Does one side of the room feel overly heavy? If so, try to adjust. If the room is sparsely furnished, you may need to toss the idea of balance out the window. You can only really balance a room properly if there is sufficient amount of furnishings to fill the entire room. Since this is counter to the staging philosophy, balancing an entire room is not as essential as making sure the arrangements themselves IN the room are balanced and appealing to the eye, directing the buyer's eye where you want it to focus upon.

Uneven Numbers – Generally speaking, groupings of furniture feel best when there are odd numbers. The same rule applies to accessories on a table. In most situations, have the seller arrange the accessories in groupings of odd numbers (1, 3, 5). Tell the seller not to put more than 5 accessories in a grouping. That may even be too many for a staged home. One to three is ideal.

Here is where scale becomes important as well. Accessories grouped together should, in most cases, have assorted heights and the reduction in height should be broken into thirds. If there a lamp on a table, the plant next to it should be 2/3rds the height of the lamp, and the candle next to both of them should be 2/3rds the height of the plant. Each reduction in height is approximately a 1/3rd increment for best results. Picture an invisible triangle formed by the top of each element.

Direction – It is important to guide the eye in a certain direction, generally toward the center of a grouping, whether located on a wall or a table. Many selections of art, table or shelf ornaments "face" right or left. If you are including a right or left facing object (such as a figurine or picture for the wall), always place it so that the direction points toward the center of the grouping or into the room. If you place it facing the outer edges of the grouping, you may experience a balance issue. Direct the eye into the room, not out of it.

Chapter 21
Understanding Furniture Arrangements

Focal Points

Focal points are usually those parts of a room where the eye is naturally drawn first upon entering. Typical focal points that are created architecturally are: a fireplace, a great bay window, a built-in entertainment center and so forth. In most cases you'll want to advise the seller to place the furniture so that it faces the room's natural focal point. This must also be coordinated with the typical usage of the room. For instance, will the room be primarily used for watching TV or for eating or for enjoying a warm fire on cold nights? Will the room be used for multiple major functions? Does the room have more than one focal point?

When staging a home, you and the seller should agree on the room's focal point and where you want to most direct the buyer's attention. Ideally you'll want to place the furniture in such a manner to enhance the focal point. By doing this, the room should look purposeful, balanced and be functional all at the same time.

Traffic Lanes

Here are some general rules for traffic patterns. You always want to have the seller make sure to have enough clearance so that the room is both functional and safe, especially since people unfamiliar to the layout will be wandering through the rooms with their attention focused on things other than where they are walking (or might have small children with them).

- For major traffic paths, leave four to six feet open.
- For minor traffic paths, leave one foot-four inches to four feet open.
- To have foot room between seating area and the edge of the coffee table, leave at least one foot.
- Leave 3 feet of space behind a recliner if placing in front of a wall or traffic lane unless it is a wall hugger.
- For foot and leg room in front of a chair or sofa, leave 1-1/2 feet to 2-1/2 feet open.
- Leave three feet open in front of a piano chair or bench.
- For occupied chairs, allow two feet per person left open.
- Leave 2 feet to three feet as the open space to get into chairs.
- Leave 1-1/2 feet to two feet of open traffic path around the table and occupied chairs.
- For making a bed, leave 1-1/2 to 2-1/2 feet open around a bed.
- Between twin beds, leave a traffic path of between 1-1/2 feet to 2-1/3 feet open.
- In front of dressers, leave at least three feet of walk space to allow you to open the drawers.

Have the seller mark down the room's measurements and note the traffic flow for the room. Then advise seller to take the measurements of the major pieces of furniture in the room that will be staying. You don't have to measure any furniture that will be leaving the premises, only if it will be used somewhere in the home.

The only measurements they will really need to take are the length and width. Occasionally they might need to measure the height of something. Jot down on their paperwork the name of the furniture and its measurements and what room it is currently in or what room it will be moved to. As the seller begins to work and try to decide if a certain piece will fit a certain place, measurements will all be readily available and should be double checked first before moving something, particularly if it is heavy. Advise the seller to remove all antiques or cherished hand-me-downs or luxury furnishings from the home. See Chapter 26 for my steel furniture lifter set, which includes carpet and floor sliders to make furniture moving easy and safe.

Most Common Configurations

There are certain types of furniture arrangements or configurations that are common and should be easily utilized by the seller when arranging a living room or family room. While there are always exceptions, most rooms of any size should be able to accommodate a configuration from this basic list (there will be exceptions, however, so further design training should be acquired than what is included in this book). By studying the traffic lanes of the room and the size and shape of the room, the proper configuration should be recognizable, even by a novice. Here are four of the most common configurations that your seller could consider depending on the type of furniture available.

In most cases, the sofa should be brought out into the room facing the focal point, but in smaller rooms this might not be possible. But sellers should be encouraged to use the center of the room whenever possible and not rely on pushing the sofa up against a wall. Interior designers and professional home stagers tend to use the middle of the room which allows for better traffic flow, a more intimate and conversational arrangement and the ability to maximize the room's perceived spaciousness.

The L-shaped Configuration

The L-shaped configuration is usually formed with a sofa and a loveseat, or a sofa with a couple of matching chairs placed perpendicular to the sofa. In this example, the sofa is against the wall as the room is small. The open part of the L should face the main entrance to the room, if possible. This does not obstruct easy travel within the room and welcomes buyers to enter the room.

The U-shaped Configuration

The U-shaped configuration extends the L-shaped configuration by closing up one of the two remaining sides of the arrangement, forming the shape of a "U". While this arrangement accommodates more furniture, it should be used with care and only in a very large room or great room. The last thing you want your seller to do is to make a room look and feel very small, so the use of furniture in a room should be kept rather sparse.

Here you can see that there is seating on 3 sides, four if you count the ottomans. While this room is beautifully arranged for someone living in the room, it is probably too much furniture to have in the room when staging. Remove the ottomans. Always remember, advise your sellers to be stingy with how much they place in the room. In staging, less is usually more.

The H-shaped Configuration

In this configuration, the major seating pieces are placed opposite each other. A coffee table is placed between the two sets of chairs to serve both sides. This type of arrangement really enhances conversation and keeps a room looking cozy and comfortable. This configuration is often used when a seller has two matching sofas of equal length.

The Angled Configuration

The angled configuration is a more complex arrangement. It is usually reserved for spaces where the room's natural focal point is angled. For instance, if the fireplace is situated on an angled wall, it would be appropriate to angle the sofa as well to face the fireplace. If there is a TV in a room where there also is a fireplace, it is ideal to place the TV near the fireplace and angle the seating arrangement so that it can focus on both the TV <u>and</u> the fireplace at the same time. In the picture above, the focal point is the view out the back windows. The loveseat has been angled to draw a buyer's eyes to the focal point. An "L-shaped" arrangement could also have been effectively used in this situation.

Many stagers like to angle dining room sets for an unusual effect. But many sellers own round or octagonal dining room sets. The placement of the chairs can give the illusion of being angled in the room and should be a definite consideration as seen below.

While there are many more configurations that professional stagers use when arranging furniture (covered in depth in our courses and other books), you should find that in most cases one of these four configurations will be perfect for the seller to use to bring any room into conformity with good design concepts and yet keep the room open and spacious at the same time.

Vignettes

Vignettes are small furniture or accessory arrangements that are meant to suggest ideas or purposes for a room. They in no way fill up a room in the sense one would fill a room if one was decorating the room for a permanent resident. They are economical ways to give an empty room some personality to help a buyer see the room's potential usage without having to decorate it more fully. Vignettes are handy to use in the less important rooms such as: children's bedrooms, home offices, attics, laundry rooms, sewing rooms or any room if the budget is extremely tight.

For instance, a vignette might consist of a desk and chair placed in a small bedroom suggesting the room could also be used as a home office rather than a bedroom.

A vignette might consist of a sewing machine on a small table with a chair suggesting a room could be used as a crafts or sewing room.

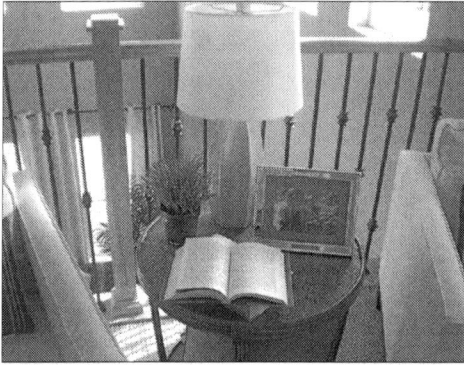

A vignette might be a grouping of chairs with a table between on the landing at the top of the stairs to suggest an intimate reading area.

A vignette might consist of some weight machines near an exercise mat suggesting the room could be a home gym rather than a bedroom.

A chair with a beach towel and a basket of magazines could suggest a sun deck where one could grab a quick tan and read, for instance.

A vignette can be any type of grouping of pieces that look good together that can fill a corner of a room or to enhance the focal point. Vignettes generally are simple and easy to pull together.

A wise agent will look for ideas to pass on to the seller to give the rooms a wide arrange of purposes so that buyers don't automatically assume every room has to be a bedroom unless they need multiple bedrooms for a large family.

Before and After Pictures

Most homes occupied by sellers, who are not in the design business or who have not hired an interior designer to decorate, will need help in the area of furniture arrangement. It's not that sellers have poor taste (some do), but most have not been trained in the art of placing furniture and accessories, so they just guess at it. If there is furniture in the house, it's going to need to be properly arranged and you must make the seller understand that there are specific ways furniture <u>should</u> be arranged to enhance the home and draw the buyers into the room.

On the following pages are some **simple** examples to show you the difference between poor arrangements and better arrangements so any seller can make <u>even the smallest of improvements</u> with your advice.

Before Decluttering

After decluttering

Before Accessorizing

After Accessorizing

Before Replacements

Bathroom1 Before

After Replacements

Bathroom1 After

Before Furnishing

After Furnishing

Before Rearranging

After Rearranging

Chapter 22
Understanding Accessory Arrangements

Use of Plants

Most sellers have few plants and often they are very small and unhealthy. Encourage your sellers to make use of plants, whether artificial or real. A garden-like vignette can help bring the outdoors inside, giving a room a special ambiance.

But like anything else, care should be taken not to overdo a good thing. If live plants are used, they must receive tender, regular care throughout the duration of the showing of the home. There are few things as distasteful to buyers as dead or dying plants.

Table Arrangements

End tables and consoles (sofa tables) are a nice place for a few accessories,

particularly in a living room, family room or bedroom. But end tables are often overly crowded and sellers should be advised to keep the decorations to a minimum.

If a table grouping is chosen, the arrangement should be limited to no more than 3 pieces (odd numbers generally work best for balance). In staging you want to suggest possibilities but sellers should beware of going overboard as they tend to do when decorating to stay.

Notice here that a simple arrangement of accessories on the console behind the sofa has added an extra element of surprise and interest. Keep this to a real minimum.

Mantels

Mantels go part and parcel with a fireplace, which is usually the focal point of a room. Therefore they are important to the room and should be decorated nicely. But advise your seller away from making the mantel decoration too elaborate. Here the wisest choice was to leave the mantel bare.

In modern settings, less is generally far better than decoration at all. Notice how simply this modern room has been decorated. There is no pretention. There is nothing that detracts. All attention goes to the architecture yet the room welcomes the buyer and suggests a huge amount of openness and spaciousness.

Dining Room Tables

A strong centerpiece that mirrors the shape of the table is a quick and easy way to dress up a dining room table. So if the table is round, the centerpiece should be round as well, or at least give the appearance of being round. A centerpiece should look good from all sides. Since there will actually be no dinner party, it doesn't matter if the centerpiece is tall or not. As a matter of fact, if the dining room has a vaulted ceiling, a tall centerpiece is just the element to bring attention to the height of the room, making it feel even more spacious and grand.

Coffee Tables

Ornamentation for the coffee table doesn't need to be elaborate but it should be color coordinated and in keeping with the style of the room and the scale of the coffee table. By using accessories that blend with the room's color palette, the seller should find it relatively easy to repeat colors around the room, bringing a sense of harmony and unity to the space.

Placement of Art

Placement of art is one of the most misunderstood concepts in decorating. The average homeowner hangs their pictures much too high. Perhaps because it is a job that often falls to the man of the house. Often people think the art should be hung in the center of the left over wall. Wrong!

Art should always be hung at eye level, which is typically 5' 6". When it is hung over furniture, such as a sofa, it is important to hang it low enough so that when viewed together with the sofa, they appear as one, not two separate entities.

Companions should be hung side by side in most cases unless in a stairwell. The base of the art should be approximately a hand span from the top of the furniture below it. In most cases this would be approximately 4-10 inches maximum.

Whether hanging a single work of art or companions, the width of the art should extend 2/3rds the width of the sofa or furniture below it (remember the 1:1.6 rule?). To exceed this measurement will undoubtedly make the art feel top heavy. In the following example, the art is "pushing it" and feels a bit top heavy. But I wanted to show you this example because I want you to notice how close the base of the art is to the top of the sofa. This is the proper way to hang art over a sofa. You do not need to be afraid that people will bang the back of their heads on the art. The depth of the sofa will prevent that from happening (unless you have kids who are out of control in the space – and then you have other problems).

Chapter 23
Understanding
Enhancement Tricks

Front Yard

Long before a
buyer sees the
inside of a home,
they will see the
exterior, usually
from the curb or
from across the
street. This is why
the front yard and
driveway are
vitally important.
If you cannot
attract a buyer to get out of the car and walk up the driveway
or steps and get to the front door and want to walk inside,
the sale has already been lost. Make sure the home looks
neat and inviting from the sidewalk first and foremost. Don't
let your seller shoot themselves in the foot by
underestimating the value of great curb appeal. Have them
leave the front lights on day and night.

Entry

The entry sets the stage for the entire home, so it is a very important area. It needs to feel welcoming and spacious. It should have some personality but only enough to beckon the buyer to explore the home further.

Living Room

An extremely dramatic area rug really adds drama to this room but will not turn off buyers because it is not permanent. For many people a living room is reserved just for company while most of the actual "living" is done in the family room. But it is still a very important part of the home. Buyers will be looking for spaciousness, perhaps a view, perhaps a fireplace or other strong architectural element that gives it some character and uniqueness.

So you'll want to advise your seller to enhance whatever natural assets the home has, particularly in the rooms the buyer will view first. This will generate more excitement to see the rest of the home. The longer a buyer stays in the home, looking around, the greater the chances are they will make an offer.

Here is where good placement of furniture becomes critical. Some people may tell you that you should place furniture in such a way to force the buyer to move in a particular direction or to look in a certain direction. I advise caution about this sort of advice. If it makes the room look or feel unattractive, it is not worth it. You don't want the room to look contrived or manipulated or out of balance.

The buyer needs to feel instantly that the room has been arranged for the family living there to use in a functional way. They also need to be impressed with the way the room looks by how it is arranged. If you have advised the seller to place the furniture or accessories in an odd manner in hopes you'll draw the buyer's attention in a specific direction, you may very well defeat the whole goal of creating a functional and beautiful room. Believe me – buyers will find their own way to the outside or the other rooms. They do NOT need the seller to overly manipulate their appreciation of the home.

Family Room

Here is a great example of a U-shaped configuration created by combining two sofas with two matching club chairs. The family room usually sports a TV, and nowadays it's usually a giant TV or a TV in a very large entertainment center. If there is a TV present, you must advise the seller to arrange the furniture facing either the TV or a fireplace (if one is present). Ideally they should be located near each other so that the seating arrangement faces both at the same time. If there is no TV or fireplace, there might be some fabulous windows with a great view. By placing the furniture it is possible to enhance the view while showing great ideas for how the room could be used.

In a great room, it will probably be necessary to advise the seller to split the room into sections and arrange seating for each section. While it is important to let buyers know how spacious a great room is, it is equally important to let them know how useful the space can be and how they might incorporate the room for many tasks, not just for watching TV.

Kitchen

One of the most important rooms in the home (in particular to the person who cooks meals), the kitchen should receive prime attention by the seller. This room will sell the home in many cases. It should be updated, if possible and should be extremely clean and neat. It should be void of stains, spills, grease, oil, or any kind of messiness.

Advise the seller to remove nearly everything in the kitchen, leaving only some bare essentials to decorate the counters and island, if it has one. Utilitarian items should be removed or stored out of sight. The counters should be completely bare save for a few decorative items.

Dining Room

Dining rooms do not need to be fully decorated at each place

setting as if one is expecting guests to arrive at any minute. However, if the dining room is large and table is large, it might be good to decorate the whole table so that buyers can quickly see how many guests they will be able to accommodate when they choose to entertain.

The centerpiece and the tableware selected should be tasteful and in good scale to the table. While it does not need to look as plush as pictured here, with a little attention to detail your seller can surely come up with a table setting that is attractive. Notice flatware is <u>not</u> recommended for security purposes.

Master Bedroom

Understandably the master bedroom is also a key room that buyers will care about. They will be looking for spaciousness, particularly if they have a large bed already. They may be concerned about noise and lighting and how far or close the master is to the other bedrooms.

If the master suite is large, it is important to include a queen sized bed in the room rather than a king. By reducing the number of other furnishings in the room, your seller will reassure buyers that the room is plenty big enough for a large bed. By placing additional bedding of a different color across the foot of the bed as shown here, the bed will appear to be much wider than it actually is, fooling the eye into believing it is a king sized bed. Extra furniture in the room may be advisable, but not as crucial as having a bed in the room.

The bed, naturally, should be appointed with a decorating flair, including a beautiful bedspread, coordinating pillows and a few enhancement techniques to make it memorable. Here a lovely tray with a plant has been added at the foot of the bed for that added extra touch.

Have your seller include a notice on the tray asking buyers to refrain from sitting on the bed.

Other Bedrooms

While it is important to suggest non-adult age groups when decorating the other bedrooms, it is generally considered inadvisable to tell your seller that fancy ceilings, strong colors or strong walls should be left in tact. While this is a beautiful room, a buyer who doesn't have a teenage daughter will feel a bit overwhelmed at the thought of having to change out such a stylized room. Suggest to the seller that a room such as this be reinvented in a more neutral palette.

Bathrooms

Cleanliness is paramount to any bathroom in the home, whether it is the master bath or a secondary bath. It absolutely must be sanitary, fresh and sparkling. Filth of any kind in the bathroom can kill a sale.

But at the same time, creating a feeling of a spa or oasis can really entice a buyer to fall in love with the home. Advise your seller to pay particular attention to all of the bathrooms and make them as beautiful and spotless as possible.

Home Office

As more and more people start businesses or elect to work from home, the home office has increased in importance around the country. With so many people laid off work in a recession, many must start businesses from home to avoid government aid.

So it is more important than ever to suggest a home office in a home, even if one must repurpose a bedroom to do it. Whether the seller has a home office or not, it is advisable to suggest they find a way to incorporate a desk somewhere to suggest a home office potential. The seller should not leave it up to a buyer to "see the potential" when they can actually create a space for a home office. It does not need to be an official desk. One can create the illusion of an office with a console table and a chair if nothing else is available.

Halls

In many cases halls can be narrow, particularly in older homes. So in a narrow hall it is not advisable to have the seller hang anything up that will make the hall feel darker or crowded. Instead consider advising the seller to place some decorative item at the <u>end</u> of the hall to attract the buyer's attention, such as a tree.

Leave the walls of the hall stripped bare of art or photos, making sure the paint is pastel to give the appearance of a wide, easy to access hall way.

Stair Cases

Staircases are good places to hang some art that is tasteful, well proportioned and in keeping with the color flow of the home. If the wall is curved, you'll need to advise the seller to hang narrow works of art and to hang them in a stair-stepped fashion, following the same angle of the stairs. Companions are great. If the seller does not have anything suitable, they should consider making something or renting or borrowing something. It will add greatly to the ambience of the stairwell.

Advise the seller not to overdo it as the stairs should still feel open and airy. The more that is hung on the wall, the smaller the stairs will feel. A little goes a long way. Sellers should remove any and all family photos from stairwells and halls, or anywhere else for that matter.

Laundry

The laundry room should look sleek, clean and orderly. Removal of the hanging garments in this laundry room would be greatly advised. Instead advise your seller to put out some neatly folded towels in a basket and place on the dryer as if waiting to be carried to the linen closet. Colorful artificial flowers set on top can be a very nice touch to add.

Back Yard

Every buyer is interested in space and the more the better. So it is not surprising they should be impressed with a great backyard that is suitable for entertaining and a safe place for children to play.

Sellers can forget that the backyard is to be included in the staging of the home. Advise them to make sure all toys and tools are removed or stored away out of sight. The back yard should feel attractive to buyers. Plants should be plentiful and well groomed. Vignettes of conversation areas are always a welcome addition.

Pool

What owner doesn't dread the upkeep of a pool? This is why it is vital that the pool be maintained properly. It should be clean of debris and leaves, and all tools should be removed or stored out of sight. Make sure all lawn chairs are attractively arranged and it wouldn't hurt to display some flowers, or include a tray of faux drinks somewhere.

Advise the seller to place a couple of sun bathing towels neatly on one or two of the chairs.

Side Yards

In their haste to get everything done, a seller might easily overlook the side yards. These should be free of garden tools, trash bins, excess garbage or auto parts and so forth. A buyer should be able to explore every corner of the property and come away feeling impressed with the overall upkeep of the property. Tell your seller to never underestimate the importance of taking care of little details. Little details left unaddressed can ruin an otherwise great review by the buyers.

Garage

The garage should, if at all possible, be emptied completely. The floors must be in great condition, minus auto residue, and it should be swept clean and all cobwebs and trash removed.

Remind the seller that the garage is still important to the whole story even though people do not live in it. There are many buyers who will pay attention to the garage because they might use the area for crafts or for a bonus play area for their children or even a home office.

Attic/Basement

There are many parts of the country where homes do not include attics or basements. However, there are many places where they are common place. Often times these spaces are dark and musty.

Encourage your seller to address these areas too. Odors can really be a turn off to buyers and the sellers might not even realize that they have an offensive smell, particularly in these spaces. It will take brutal frankness on your part to make them aware so they can take steps to correct the problem.

Odors can come from pets, paints, garbage and trash, mold, mildew and other contaminates. Advise the seller to not rely solely on room deodorants that may just mask the smells, but they may need to take more drastic actions to eliminate offensive odors.

Chapter 24
Understanding Other
Important Criteria

Cleaning

It should be common sense that a house be thoroughly cleaned before putting it up for sale but it is shocking the number of sellers who don't use their God-given common sense. Be that as it may, agents need to push sellers to make sure the house is clean – as spotless as possible, particularly in the bathrooms and kitchen.

Besides one's own efforts, sellers can hire professional stagers or cleaning companies to get a home spotless. Since they work with more powerful cleaning products, I think this is a MUST, but some sellers may feel confident to clean the property in a professional manner.

Cleaning efforts should include making the home void of smells that turn off buyers. Sellers should look to third parties that don't live in the home to check the home for smells.

Repairs and Replacements

Most homes need repairs of some kind. Whether it is a major repair or lots of minor repairs, repairing broken items in the home is also a must. Wouldn't it be better to take care of repairs before a home inspector requires them anyway? Repairs might involve some or all of the following: carpets, floors, brick work, wall surfaces, plumbing, electrical, yard work, picture frames, pottery, dead plants, roofs, woodwork, hardware and so forth.

As you preview a property, you should note the level of repairs that will be necessary to see if simple free consultation advice from you will be enough to address the problems. If in doubt, push the seller to hire a professional stager. The fees a stager will charge will most definitely be less than the cost of a major price reduction.

Acquisition of Additional Furnishings

It is no secret that furnished homes sell easier than unfurnished homes. They also tend to sell for higher prices as well. So it is incumbent upon you as the listing agent to urge any seller with an unfurnished property to seek out furnishings that can be used while the home is on the market. Perhaps they have furniture they can put back in the home or furniture they can borrow from a relative or friend.

Many professional stagers have their own inventory that they provide to sellers on a monthly rental basis to make sure the property is presented in its best light. If a stager is hired who does not have inventory, furnishings can always be rented from a rental company. Terms of rental companies vary but it is not unusual to have a 3-month minimum contract requirement. One of the advantages is that the rental company will deliver and pick up the furniture they rent making the process quite easy for the seller, particularly if they are out of the area at the time the house is staged and shown.

One of the advantages of using the services of a professional stager is that they will be able to determine what types of furnishings the home needs to show properly. This type of advice can be crucial. Most sellers will be ill-prepared to make these kinds of decisions on their own. If the right furnishings are not placed in the home in the right places, the outcome will not be as pleasing to potential buyers as it could be. Placement of the furnishings is crucial to highlight the home's assets and make each room look as spectacular as possible.

Packing and Removal

Packing up the seller's possessions is a time-consuming, tedious chore. The seller will not be looking forward to this job. A professional stager is equipped to manage this task on their behalf, however, which makes professional stagers particularly in demand and much appreciated.

One thing is clear. It needs to be done at some point, so better to encourage the seller to accomplish it as soon as possible. Boxes should be labeled and stored elsewhere. Storing boxes in the garage is ok in an emergency, but ideally all stored items should be completely removed from the property.

Storage boxes can be purchased from packing and mailing supply companies and from moving companies. Home stagers usually have their sources for boxes, labels and pods and can greatly assist in providing quick and convenient storage options.

Storage

If the seller does not have a local relative or friend who can help them out when storing their removed property during the selling process, they can rent a storage space with such companies as Public Storage. Public storage often runs ads advertising the first month's storage at $1.00, making it an economical place for short term storage needs.

Some stagers will have discount coupons for Pods, a moveable storage unit, the Pods company will bring to the property for loading boxes. When the pod is full, the company comes and gets it and stores the Pod in their facility until the seller has sold the property. This can be an option for sellers to help make sure removed items are secured safely.

Professional home stagers will be helpful to sellers in determining what items need to be removed from the premises. Typically one would not keep utilitarian furnishings in the home. If they are kept, sellers are urged to keep them out of sight.

Redesign Services

If a seller is moving into a different home in the local area, they will possibly have a need for help in arranging their furnishings in their new space. In addition to this, the buyer of your seller's property may also need help at some point arranging their furnishings in your seller's home after escrow closes.

For this reason, professional stagers usually offer redesign services as well and will be only too happy to work with the seller and the buyer in getting their homes beautifully arranged after escrow. When seeking a professional stager, look for one who is adept at redesign services to get the most help possible on the front and back end.

Stagers will often offer additional services such as: color consultation, floral arrangement design, holiday decorating, wall grouping design, packing and unpacking services, photographic services, garage sale services, video services and more.

I am sometimes asked whether the staging should reflect the time of year and any holidays coming up. My answer is that holiday decorating should be incorporated sparingly when staging and should be as generic as possible unless the seller is adamant about it being quite specific for some reason. With decorations such as pictured here, no one would take offense for religious reasons. But this is an individual choice each seller should make for themselves. Clearly the agent should not make the decisions in this case.

Chapter 25
When Home Stagers Are Crucial to Success

When You Should Defer to Professional Home Stagers

Offering free staging advice to a seller is admirable and will be appreciated in most every case. But it is important to keep in mind that free advice will likely be received with less impact than consultation that is fee based by a stager. As human beings, we tend to have less respect for that which we get for free. So don't be too surprised if your free advice gets ignored or reduced to bare essentials.

If your free advice is getting ignored or you can't get the seller to act in a timely manner, or the scope of the needs of the house are significant, free staging advice (no matter how good it is) will not be enough. Time is money. And even if you are highly motivated and love the concept of staging and helping the seller save money, it will not be in their best interest to limp along and get little of the essential work done.

My sister's daughter and husband wanted to sell their home. They were in financial trouble and needed to get it sold as soon as possible.

But left to their own devices, they lost far more in the long run than if they would have hired a professional stager. Houses were on the decline but this wasn't enough motivation to get the seller working on the property.

The wife took the kids and moved 3 hour's drive away to live with relatives, leaving the husband at the property to fix problems and get it ready for market. While there was furniture left in the home, the husband had no clue how to arrange it. Instead of jumping in and tackling the problem and getting the job done, the husband dilly dallied for 6 months, bringing tears to his wife's eyes each time she visited to see what had been accomplished – or rather what had not.

In the end, the house finally went on the market – well below market, and the house was sold short leaving the family still owing on the mortgage and losing all their equity. Costs invested were also a total loss though without them the house would have sold for an even lower price adding to the seller's deficit.

Had the home been staged in less than 30 days by a professional, it would have probably made the seller a profit – or at least mitigated their damages. Knowing what to do and being motivated to do it are two different things. This guide will go a long way to help you give free advice that is extremely helpful, but it may not be sufficient to help a seller do an all-out staging service of their own.

A wise agent will know when to back off and pull in professional services to get the job done right.

How to Find Local Professional Stagers

The old fashioned method for finding a professional stager was to look them up in your local telephone book. But times have changed. Now the majority of agents and sellers hunt for stagers online.

There are two ways to accomplish a thorough search:

1. Look in the online directories of training companies who teach home staging. A simple search under the phrase "home staging" should produce a significant number of training companies, mine among them. Toward the end of this chapter I'll give you the links to the two professional directories I host on two of my websites or you can simply find them by going to my website, Decorate-Redecorate.Com.

2. The second way is to enter the phrase "home staging" or "home stagers" PLUS your city and state into the search phrase of your favorite search engine. Google's local search should present you with one or more local home stagers but you'll probably discover the websites or directory pages of professional stagers who are in your state or even in your home town by doing a more targeted local search.

Collect the contact information of several stagers local to your seller and make contact with them. Look for stagers with great communication skills and enthusiasm. If there is something over the phone that concerns you right away, do not move forward to interview that person (unless they are the only person you find within reasonable distance to help your seller). If you have several names to choose from, interview at least three or suggest all of the names to the seller to interview.

You'll find there may be a wide variety of methods and pricing structures between full service stagers. Some of this is due to how they were trained and some of this is due to experience and level of expertise or other unknown factors. Choosing the least expensive is always tempting but could be costly to the seller (or to you) if that person is too inexperienced or lacks knowledge or talent. A good rule of thumb is to look closely at the stager whom the seller can best relate to and who, hopefully, falls somewhere in the middle when it comes to pricing.

Questions to Ask a Home Stager

Since it is important to get to know any home stager you might recommend to the seller, you'll want to interview them carefully to determine which professional will best serve the needs of the seller. So here is a brief list of questions you might consider asking a professional home stager.

1. How long have you been staging homes?
2. Is home staging your primary focus or do you have other services you also offer? What are those services?
3. Did you attend a seminar, class, or workshop? When, where and with whom?
4. What is their training and background?
5. Did you take a home study course?
6. Who trained you and what is their background or reputation in the industry?
7. Did you earn a designation from your trainer? Do you have a certificate of completion I can see?
8. Were you given a designation after attending a seminar for a couple of days or did you have to take and pass an exam as part of the requirements to become certified?
9. Did you need to submit a portfolio of your early work to the trainer for review and evaluation before getting their designation or was there no accountability required of you?
10. Did your training include interior design concepts or just business concepts and positive thinking?
11. Do you work part time or full time?
12. May I see examples of homes you have staged previously?
13. Do you have a list of testimonials of satisfied home owners and/or other agents you can give me?
14. May I contact any of the agents or sellers you have worked for in the past for a testimonial?

15. Do you do all the work yourself or do you have a staff?
16. Do you hire third party entities to manage all or some of the tasks or do you do everything yourself?
17. Do you carry liability insurance?
18. What are your terms of service?
19. May I see a copy of your typical contract?
20. Do you work on a flat fee or an hourly rate?
21. If an hourly rate, what is your hourly rate?
22. Do you require a minimum number of hours?
23. How are your flat fees calculated?
24. If the seller is under a tight schedule, how free are you to manage the project and complete the work by their deadline?
25. Are your helpers your employees or independent contractors?
26. Why should the seller select you as the home stager instead of one of your competitors?
27. Do you guarantee your work? What is your guarantee?
28. Do you have your own inventory to stage the seller's home or do you rent furniture and props or require the seller or agent to do so?
29. Do you request a minimum rental period? If so, what is the minimum?
30. Do you have a list of all the services your business includes?
31. Do you have a list of all the services your business does *not* include?
32. Will you be at the project all or most of the time to supervise if you are using employees or independent contractors or are you merely the salesperson?
33. Have you collected current copies of the liability insurance and business licenses (and contractor's licenses, if any) of all third party entities you plan to use on a project? Can you provide such documentation to the seller upon request?

Obviously this is not a complete list, but it will help guide you to get the most important specifics from the stager. You can compile the data for each stager you are considering and pass the information on to the seller, or sift through the information yourself and make only one recommendation to the seller.

For liability reasons, I suggest you pass all the information you have gathered on to the seller and let the seller pick the stager of their choice. Giving free advice to the seller is one thing. But you should know that when professional services are sought, it's probably in your best interest (unless you are picking up the tab) to let the seller make all final decisions and drop you out of the loop.

If you are choosing to make recommendations of one or more stagers to the seller, it is advisable to have the stagers sign a brief document that states that any services they provide will be governed by an independent contract between stager and seller. It should state that the stager agrees that you are not to be held accountable in any manner for reimbursement for services rendered. Have the stager sign and date the document.

Likewise, when you give your recommendations to the seller, you should also have the seller sign a document stating that any services the stager provides to the seller are governed by the contract between seller and stager and that you bear no responsibility or liability whatsoever. Have the seller sign and date the document.

Should a disagreement or contract dispute arise later between the stager and the seller, you do not want to be in the loop – either financially or otherwise. Sometimes, in our litigious society, one disgruntled party may try to bring other outside parties into a dispute or legal action claiming they suffered because of a recommendation provided to them. You definitely want to make sure it doesn't happen to you simply because you made any recommendations that benefited either party or were costly to any party.

Online Staging Directories

I offer two online directories where you'll find thousands of stagers and/or re-designers across the USA, Canada and as far away as Australia and Europe (but there are many other directories on the web as well). Almost every member in my directories has taken training in one form or another directly from the eBooks and books that I have written or courses I have developed. While every attempt is made to keep the directories current and relevant, we cannot accept responsibility for errors, nor for those members who do not keep us up-to-date with their contact information.

Please remember all members of my directories are independent entities and are solely responsible for the claims and representations they make and enter into. We provide the directory merely as a means of connecting sellers, agents and stagers together and are not responsible for any transactions, nor do we profit in any way from any transactions that may take place. Due diligence is required of anyone seeking the services of members in the directory.

The Diamond Directory

The Diamond Directory includes only professional stagers who have taken a course at a Gold or Diamond level. While I cannot vouch for each business listed, I can only assume they invested quality time and effort into studying the extensive material they were provided. And because they invested seriously into their training, I have separated them out from the rest into a more exclusive directory of their own. You'll find them here under the state of their residence:

http://www.homestaging4profit.com/directory.html

The General Directory

While the vast majority of members of this directory have purchased some type of business training from the ebooks and books I have published, this list also contains a few people who were trained elsewhere but purchased a listing in the directory. This list will include many, many stagers who took training elsewhere and were dissatisfied with the content of what they got - so they purchased additional training from my website.

This directory will also include a few individuals who have purchased training in the corporate art consulting industry. Their listings are shown with an "A" after the phone number. Many stagers listed in the general directory have achieved their professional designations of CSS or CRS (or both) after completing the certification process. They had to pass a 75 question exam and submit a portfolio of their work in order to achieve our highly coveted designations. Many of these individuals are highlighted in red boxes in the directory to salute their extraordinary efforts and proven talents. Obviously our certified members have earned the right to be singled out for special recognition and should have a Certificate of Achievement in their portfolio to show you during any interview process.

http://www.decorate-redecorate.com/directory/directory.html

Chapter 26
Where to Find Additional Staging Training & Tools

Courses You Can Take

Many real estate agents decide at some point that they are more interested in serving clients as professional stagers rather than continuing as agents. After reading this book, you may feel that way as well. Since the material I cover in this book is only a portion of what professional stagers typically learn, anyone considering a career change is advised to take additional training in the design and business structures needed for success as professional stagers running a business.

Training opportunities now abound – some good and some not so good. In all matters, take time to investigate before choosing.

There are, of course, seminars and workshops available. They usually require your attendance for 5 days. Prices are dramatically higher for this type of "hands-on" training and, depending on your location, you might have to travel considerable distance to attend and pay for lodging while there. Typically when taking a seminar, you'll be required to sign an agreement to abide by the association's rules (which may easily infringe on your independence) and there are usually hefty annual renewal fees you'll have to pay. The quality of the seminar and the training is dependent on who conducts the seminar, not its founder. Many do not include design training as part of the seminar, claiming staging is not decorating and part of the real estate industry not the design industry. But facts are facts and failure to teach design dramatically weakens a stager's effectiveness out in the field.

There are also online, web-based courses or combination-style courses (such as my own – consisting of eBooks, books, visual aids, tools and online training). Some require you to take all of the training online with strict deadlines and there are always hefty annual fees to pay to retain access to the training and anything associated with it (like a website). Some offer design training and some do not. For myself, I decided early on to be **student centered** first and foremost, so I do _not_ charge renewal fees for training. The only forward going fees I charge are for website renewals because I am charged renewal fees by the third party entities that host the websites. These fees are minimal, however.

Again it is important to investigate your options thoroughly before choosing the training style that is right for you. It is also important to investigate the reputation of the trainers to see how long they have been in business, their company's Better Business Bureau rating, their testimonials, their designations, whether they provide design training or not, their visual aids, tools and so forth. You want to make sure the company you train with has an excellent reputation and, if seeking a designation, offers a designation that enjoys the highest respect. Notice I did not say the designation that is the most well known. Being well known should not be the major criteria for determining quality, integrity and respect.

For those interested in my highest value course as of this writing, please visit this webpage for complete details:

http://www.decorate-redecorate.com/diamond-ruby-combo-course.html

This course includes comprehensive training in the home staging AND interior re-design industries for anyone wishing to start their own business. It will solidify your confidence in both design and business structure, provide you with essential visual aids that will help you promote your business from day one, and provide you with extremely handy tools that make furniture movement super easy. The course includes a student's certification fee, a lifetime access to the Diamond private training website, two lifetime directory listings, a brochure website, newsletters, personal advice, a discussion forum, your own personal reference library, some valuable eBooks and much, much more. Please note, this course is subject to change without notice. For the most up-to-date information on anything I offer, please visit my website.

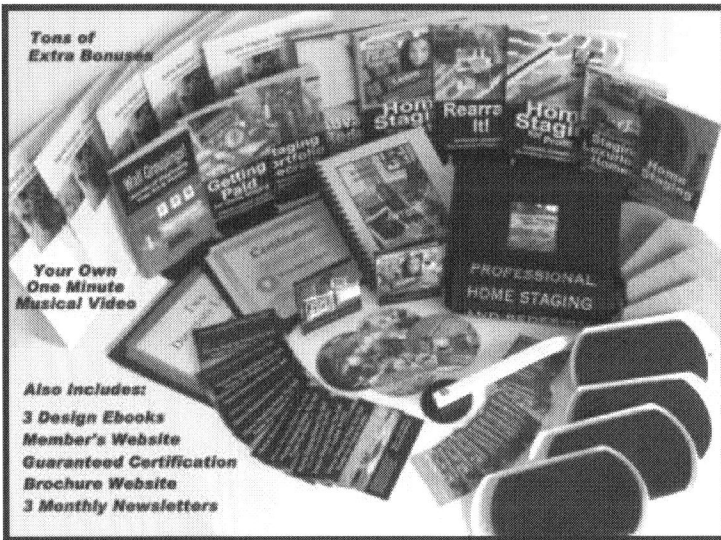

Books You Can Acquire

For many, taking advantage of a course offers the highest degree of comprehensive training and support and the most value for their investment. They would be right. However, not everyone has the resources or time to take this route. Happily there are other options. Below are a listing of ebooks and books that I have written which are also available "a la carte" for your convenience. Full details are available on each one at my website so I'll only provide a brief snippet here.

Business Training by the Author

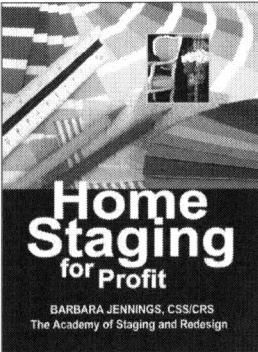

Home Staging for Profit gives readers a clear and precise guide to opening, growing and maintaining a successful home staging <u>business</u>. Some of the concepts discussed in this manual will be repeated or developed more fully in this basic training guide. But there is a huge amount of additional, in-depth training not included here, as well as extremely handy business forms, business start-up guidance and so much more. It is 256 pages of incredibly detailed how-to information in a large sized format (8.5x11) and is currently my best selling manual (also available in eBook format). For specific details please visit <u>Decorate-Redesign.Com</u>.

Home Staging in Tough Times is a sequel to the book above. It was developed at the onset of our economic recession and is packed full of guidance on how to survive and grow a staging business during down markets. It has many actual examples of marketing tactics and strategies readers can use, a plethora of forms to make the process easier and approaches staging from a completely different

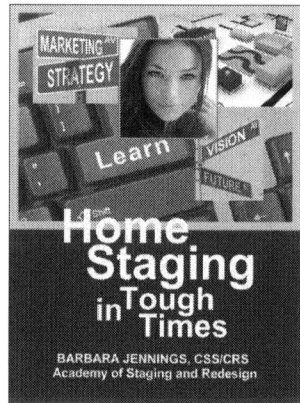

mindset one would normally use. It too is a large format manual (8.5x11) and consists of 212 pages. No one else offers this type of training unless they learned it from this book.

Staging Luxurious Homes is for professional stagers who want to specialize in upper class homes and working with agents who serve affluent neighborhoods. It is packed with details about the different ways wealthy people think and act, how to network with them, how to serve them, and how to grow a staging business as a confident professional within this specialized group. This 228 page guide is unique in the industry and comes in a 6x9 format.

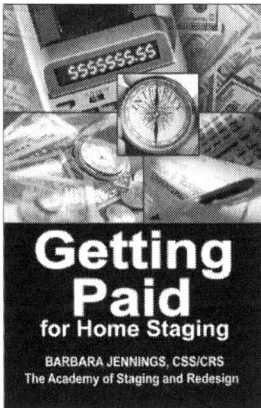

Getting Paid for Home Staging focuses on how to protect a staging business from unscrupulous consumers, who try to avoid paying for services after they have been rendered. It is a layman's look at steps anyone can take to minimize trouble before it starts. It covers staging ethics, tricks of the trade to enhance a home and much more. It is offered in a 6x9 format and is 192 pages of great protective training.

Staging Portfolio Secrets offers step by step procedures in creating a powerful, unique and in-depth staging and redesign portfolio that will help readers gain new clients. It is highly applicable to agents as well. It helps readers decipher their most engaging and useful talents from their past and present, and add them to the mix of photos, certificates, statistics and other

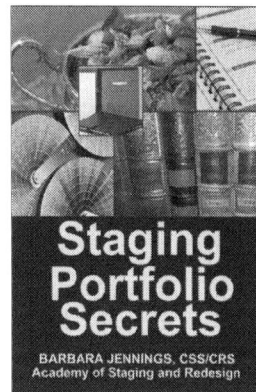

valuable data that should be part of every portfolio – the kind of information that easily sets the reader ahead of the competition. This 264 page manual in 6x9 format includes many forms, photo examples and more.

The Best Consultation Aid

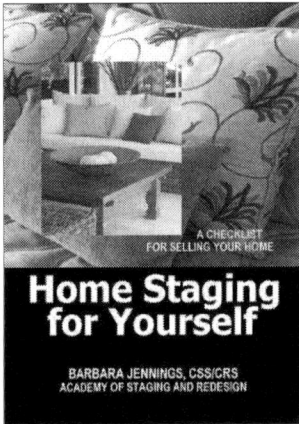

Home Staging for Yourself is an incredibly handy consultation aid for both you and your seller. It is the most thorough checklist ever developed to assist an agent, a stager or a seller inspect and compile a list of tasks that need to be addressed for every conceivable part of a home, both inside and outside. Written to the seller, each area or room of a typical home is separated out and the most common tasks that stagers address are identified for each area or room. Blank lines are also included for each room or area so that each booklet can be customized to the particular situation, making it the first and only booklet of its kind that makes organizing the vital tasks easy to follow and understand – while making the process completely customizable on the spot, saving everyone who uses it valuable time and effort. The current edition is 105 pages in size format 5x8. Stagers and agents can purchase these useful to-do lists, professionally printed in small quantities at discounted prices and pass them on to the seller for free or for a small up-charge. When up-charging for the checklist guides the guides become a small profit center for the agent or stager or a value added product offered to a seller to gain a listing. Complete details on the value and usefulness of these checklists are found in the next chapter.

Furniture Moving and Lifting Tools

No matter what your age or physical conditioning, it's important to use safety measures when moving heavy furniture to protect your spine and muscles. Should you decide to involve yourself in assisting sellers in rearranging furniture, you'll definitely appreciate acquiring several sets of **Furniture Moving sliders**. Stagers routinely use these types of tools. I advise all stagers to have several sets of carpet and floor sliders which you can get at many retailers nationwide: Home Depot, Bed Bath & Beyond to name two.

Design Training by the Author

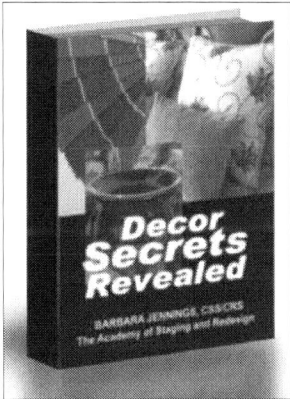

<u>Décor Secrets Revealed</u> is 25 chapters on the full scope of properly arranging furniture and accessories just like the pros. As I stated earlier, the design training in this manual covers some of the most essential concepts you should know to give great advice to sellers. However, it should be noted that it is <u>not</u> sufficient for anyone wishing to offer professional staging services. To fully learn all the tactics, rules and practices that interior designers use when arranging furniture and accessories, this electronic book is vital to your core training. It is chocked full of full color photographs (over 600) and comes in a downloadable eBook. You will learn virtually everything you need to know and then some and it will provide readers with the confidence to give solutions equal to any expert and give authoritative answers when sellers ask questions regarding furniture and accessory arrangement.

Wall Groupings! Secrets of Displaying Your Art and Photos is the sequel to a book I published in the 1980's. This 148 page book in 5x8 format is loaded with photos of all sorts of wall groupings from simple to complex. It includes all of the concepts readers should know when it comes to creating a beautifully arranged grouping, plus instructions on how to properly hang the groupings. It should be noted that this training is not especially essential for stagers and agents as staged homes generally do not include elaborate wall groupings, however it never hurts to learn this specialized training not available anywhere else.

Arrange Your Stuff

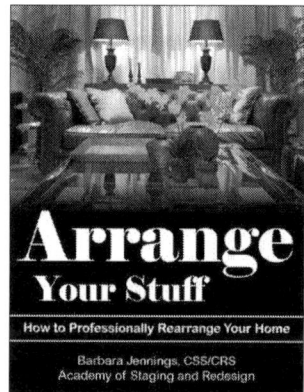

Approaching furniture arrangement concepts from a slightly different angle, my soft cover book of a wide range of sketched rooms, including the before sketch and then followed by anywhere from 1-4 sketches of how the room was and could have been arranged professionally. Lots of tips to help you immediately dissect any room and know how to solve it. Filled with the top and most common furniture arrangement configurations, you should find the answer to most rooms in these pages.   168 pages, softcover

Where to Get Our Current Training and Resource Aids and Tools

More specialized training just for real estate agents is on our agenda and in the works. For a complete list of current eBooks, books and up-to-the-minute courses (including full training in the interior re-design and corporate art consulting fields), plus all of the exclusive visual aids, tools of the trade and a huge selection of free decorating tips, please visit my flagship website:

http://www.decorate-redecorate.com

Our product catalog is located at:

http://www.decorate-redecorate.com/catalog.html

For Information About Certification

Please check our website for current information about certification <u>for agents</u> as well as professional stagers. We are currently preparing a designation (CREHSA – Certified Real Estate Home Staging Advisor) just for agents indicating an agent's qualification to offer free home staging advice. Exam and modest fee required plus proof of license in good standing. This designation does not replace, nor does it supersede, our Certified Staging Specialist (CSS) designation reserved just for professional home stagers.

Chapter 27
Benefiting From the
Home Staging Checklist
(To-Do List)

Why Is a Check List Important?

Never make the mistake that the seller will be able to successfully stage their home all on their own. You can be sure they will need advice and help. Many may have already seen TV shows about staging or even read a book. But the difficulty comes in being able to apply what they know to their own home.

First of all, they will find it difficult to separate their emotions from the tasks at hand. I've discussed this earlier. Even if they can make that transition, they will find it extremely useful and beneficial to get input from a neutral party (you or a professional stager). Since the average home needs a bit of work to properly prepare it for market, there is this cannot be accomplished without a detailed action plan.

The checklist booklet I have prepared for you and the seller is the handiest most fool-proof action plan you will ever use.

How Will a Check List Help You?

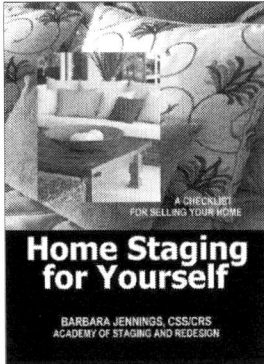

Gone is the need to write out a list on the spot. Gone is the need to return to your office to type something up for the seller. Gone is the need to rely on the seller to construct their own list. Gone is your competition when you show this pre-printed, customizable checklist to your prospective client at the time you are seeking to be their agent. Wouldn't it be incredible to figure out a way to become the listing agent every time you try?

While there are many variables that cause a seller to select one agent over another, having truly practical tips, advice, and tools at your disposal that other agents don't have is a huge advantage. Don't be one that gets left in the dust because you aren't making use of these professional checklists.

Should your competition not have such a checklist (in all likelihood they won't) they may not have thought it to be important to have. Those that have one, probably made it themselves and what they have is unlikely to be as thorough or as easy to use as what you will have.

I'm constantly amazed at the number of stagers and agents who make notes at the home, then run back to their office to type of an official "proposal" to give to the seller. It's such a waste of valuable time and so unnecessary. Don't be one of them. Time is money and the more time you can save by becoming more efficient, the better for you and your profit line.

When you hand the seller a first-class booklet, beautifully printed for them, they will see you as a true professional who is on the cutting edge of staging techniques. They will see you as someone who cares about doing things right at the outset.

They will trust you and remember you when they talk about the experience. They will be happy to refer you on to other people who want to sell their homes.

As I've stated earlier, you only get one chance to make a good first impression, and final impressions are just as powerful. But when a seller works with a professional checklist for a few days and experiences how the checklist helps them, they will never forget the experience and it will become part of their <u>lasting</u> impression of you. They may not choose to do all of the tasks that have been circled for them to address. That is their choice. But at least they will hopefully rectify the most glaring ones and you will have the satisfaction of knowing you played a key part in assisting them in getting their home sold for the highest price in the shortest time frame. They will come away from the experience singing your praises and feeling like they surely got their money's worth when they selected you to be their listing agent.

How the Check List Will Help the Seller

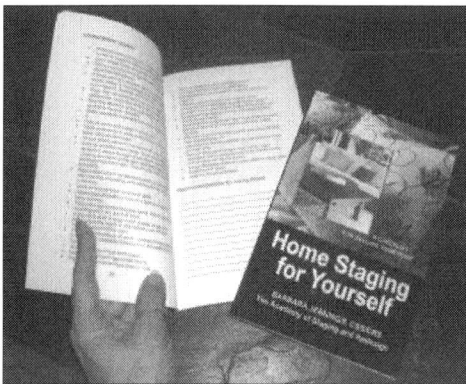

The printed checklist booklet (105 pages) is a no-nonsense, very detailed, very thorough list of every conceivable task a seller should address for every single area or room in the home and outside. There is no guess work. There is no wasted time to figure out what to check. There is no wasted time writing things down to be done at a later time. There is no chance of forgetting important things.

The checklist is a series of bulleted lists starting from the curb, moving throughout the house, ending in the back yard and side yards. It covers the curb appeal, the entry, living room, family room, kitchen, master bedroom, multiple other bedrooms, home office, laundry, halls, attic, basement, back yard and side yards. No stone is left unturned, so to speak.

All you or the seller has to do is circle the bullets that should be addressed in each section. Cross them off as the tasks are completed. If there is a custom task for a particular house, you or the seller need only write it into the booklet so it doesn't get forgotten. What could be easier? Since the booklet is professionally printed and generic enough to use in any home, the seller will be more apt to take it seriously and follow the plan that it will lay out for them. Without good follow through, your best advice will be worthless.

Using these checklists will help you help your seller to achieve maximum results when it comes to their personal staging efforts. It will help keep them on task. It will help inspire them. It will give them a professional plan to follow. It is easy to understand.

Expect them to be overwhelmed by the task ahead, especially if the house is an older home, run down, dirty, messy and presenting itself poorly. This is normal. It is also a very good time to approach them with the idea of hiring a professional stager to do it all for them. Remember, it is generally in everyone's best interest to get the staging done completely, done professionally, and done in a minimum amount of time. Many sellers will be so frazzled at the prospects of packing up and moving out and getting settled in a different location, they may be joyous at this point to turn it over to a home stager.

Support them in whatever decision gives them the most peace of mind. Only they can weigh the options and compare the value of saving some money (perhaps) by doing it themselves compared to hiring a professional. The same is true if you are planning to underwrite the services of a professional stager compared to doing more work by yourself. I stated earlier that the training you have received in this book will go a long way to guiding you to help your seller – but it is no substitute to comprehensive training that professional stagers typically get.

So try to do what is in the best interests of the seller and hopefully everyone should be extremely happy and profitable in the end.

Local Economical Shopping Tips

It is quite common for sellers to lack some of the furnishings that can make a significant difference in staging the home. Often they do not have adequate trees, plants, artwork, pillows, area rugs and large accessories. What they do have is often very small and less effective.

So if you surmise their accessories will be deficient, it is a good idea to give them a local list of places where they can shop for appropriate props. They should be low or moderately priced stores. Stores selling seconds make for good shopping experiences normally. Flea markets, swap meets and garage sales are also places to pick up inexpensive items.

By preparing a list of local shops and sources in advance, your seller will appreciate your attention to details just that much more. Pay attention to the little details and your seller will be only too happy to pass out your cards and sing your praises all the way to their own new space.

Chapter 28
Understanding the Importance of Photographs

Wide Angle Cameras

My zoom camera is a Lumix with a 12x optical zoom. It's made by Panasonic. Having said that, it's no doubt out of date by now compared to new cameras developed in the interim. My wide angle digital camera is made by Olympus and is the Camedia C-7070. They were both fairly pricey when I bought them, so don't go jump into these types of cameras until you're well on your way to an excellent career to justify the costs. I haven't tried this one, but look into the Kodak EasyShare V705 7.1MP Digital Camera with 5x Ultra-Wide-Angle Dual-Lens Optical Zoom for under $300. One staging photographer I know uses a Canon EOS 50 for outstanding photographs for the stager that hires him.

I try to take a picture of every wall in the room from the opposite side of the room. I also try to stand in every corner of the room and get a shot or two of the opposite corner. When you do this, your camera is going to pick up parts of two walls. You want to pay particular attention to getting a shot of the parts of the room you just know look "awful". You want there to be as much difference in your *before* shots from your *after* shots as possible as this will enhance your portfolio. It is the dramatic difference between the before and after that will have the greatest impression on future prospects.

Taking the "Before" Pictures

You're going to need more detailed pictures for home staging than might be typical. To back yourself up later, you're going to want to take plenty of distance shots, plenty of close ups, even take pictures of problem areas like stains, chipped paint, etc. - just load up your camera with as many pictures as you can take. You can't come back and grab more before pictures, so I always take far more than I know I will need, just as a backup. Don't rely on your memory for every detail of every room and exterior section.

If you see smaller sections of the room that need improvement (the top of a desk or table, a shelf unit or such), take close up shots of those areas. Remember what areas you took pictures of as best you can because you're going to want to try to show those areas again in the *after* shots and how your seller improved the appearance of that desk, table or shelf unit, furniture arrangement, painted wall, repaired table leg, etc. If you establish a routine early of how you take the before pictures, it should not be too hard to get to the same point of reference again when you shoot the after pictures.

You may also want to take pictures of the inside of closets, drawers, cupboards, the garage, the laundry room - places that are also important to sellers and buyers. Taking good, detailed pictures is a precautionary step as well. Should you have a problem of any kind later, you'll have plenty of proof (both before and after) to show the conditions of the home from start to finish. And you never know what you'll want to incorporate into your portfolio when all is said and done. In a nutshell, take a vast amount of pictures. Store the pictures on a CD or if you have an external drive, make backups and store there in addition to storing on your computer. I have a subscription with an online storage company that automatically backs up my pictures and critical files daily for me in their encrypted database.

Be sensitive to the seller. If the seller is busily doing something else, like cleaning or fussing with kids, etc. then you have more time to take photos, but if the seller is standing around and waiting on you, then get this part over as soon as possible.

Always keep all of your personal equipment and tools in one place out of the way while you are at the seller's home. Don't be a source of additional problems.

Once you have completed the interview process and your contract is signed to be the seller's agent, you've done your seller assisted walk-thru and you've done your private walk-through (which is where you go through the home on your own, taking the checklist booklet I described in the previous chapter with you and circling the tasks that need to be addressed, creating a custom to-do list for the seller), you are ready to begin taking pictures. Get out your camera and do that.

Explain to the seller that you always like to take "before" pictures so that you will have a reference later for both you and the seller. If you plan to use the pictures as "before and after" examples on your web site or in your literature (which I do all the time), you might also mention that you use the photos to give examples of your work to other prospective sellers in the future and add, "if that's ok with you". I've never had a client say it wasn't ok (so long as they weren't in the picture).

In case it should be a problem in the future, you can always refer back to this brief conversation confirming that you did get the seller's permission to use the photographs later.

Technically the photos are yours and part of your work product, so you really have the ability to use them however you want, but it's a nice courtesy to get their permission.

Taking the "After" Pictures

After the seller is completely done staging the home (or it is completed by a home stager), you'll want to get back in immediately to take pictures. Taking the after pictures is quite easy though great care should be taken to make sure the photos are excellent quality. Light can work against you, especially in dark areas or where there is strong backlighting from windows and doors.

As I said earlier, you'll want to repeat the process you took when photographing the home before it was staged by the seller or a professional stager. You'll want to stand in the middle of one wall and shoot the opposite wall. Then you'll want to stand in each of the four corners and shoot the opposite corner, trying to get as much of the two walls into the frame as possible.

When shooting after pictures, make sure any drapes or blinds or other window treatments are closed or nearly closed to cut down on backlighting (unless you know how to adjust your camera's settings for this). Turn all the lamps and overhead lights on to make the rooms look more cheery and to brighten dark corners. When shooting the exterior, turn all the lights on that are near the front of the home, especially if the home is in shadow or you are shooting at night. It is also a good idea to wet down the concrete or other hard surfaces in the front before shooting the photo as you'll get some amazing reflections that enhance the look of the home and make the driveway and walkways sparkle.

Always check your focus to make sure your pictures are not blurry. It's a good idea to carry a tripod at all times for low light conditions. If you are not familiar with shooting interior or exterior pictures of homes, it would be wise to visit a camera store and ask a clerk to give you some tips for your specific camera. Knowing the right settings for your camera can make a huge difference in the quality of the end product. Some agents and stagers hire professional photographers to shoot the after pictures for them or perhaps do a trade for services. It can be expensive but certainly has great advantages.

Always take more pictures that you know you will need. This may be the single time the house looks spotless and everything is in its place. Just as you can never return to grab more before pictures, you probably will not be able to return for more after pictures.

Making Videos for Online

As the use of online videos has become more economical and more widely used on the internet, it would behoove you to try to get quality video of the home and edit it for the internet. You can host the video on your website or on other websites like YouTube.

One of the drawbacks of most video cameras is that they cannot make wide angle movies. But if you know how to edit them, you can use still photos in combination with the video to give a professional appearance. While it is a lot of work, it could make a huge positive impact for both the seller and you. Any additional edge you can offer a seller will help generate additional business for you.

Tips for Making Good Pictures

Here are some do's and don'ts that will help you feature the best assets of the home after

staging and avoid the pitfalls that many agents make when shooting the outside and inside of the home.

Remember, that depending on the usage of the picture, you may only have a very small display window. For instance, if the image is to be displayed on the internet, whether on your website or another one, images must be compressed for fast downloads, so only a small postage stamp size might be available or something just slightly bigger.

So it is incumbent upon you to take several shots of the home, both outside and inside when the work is done, so that you can choose the best shot available for the method you will use to market the home.

The smaller the display area, the more difficult it is to get a really useful shot. So the closer you get the more contrast you'll get. The more illumination you have the better.

Following are some random shots that agents have taken of homes being sold. I will point out the good points or the weak points of the individual pictures so you get the idea of what will work best and what will not.

If you have concrete near the home, hose it down first with water so that when you shoot the exterior picture, you get the reflections  from the wet pavement to enhance the sparkle of the home. Be sure all the lights are on if shooting at or near dusk or at night.

If there is a nearby hill or higher place you can go to get a

shot of the house plus an attractive background, do so as in this photo. The lake and surrounding mountains near this home are big assets to it and assets like these should be included in a shot whenever possible.

Feature the home that resides on or near a cul-de-sac. That is an asset. While you're at it, include a great sunset view if you can. But don't do a distant shot like this if it diminishes special features that the home contains near the front door, because you just

can lose too much detail of what the home looks like from too far away.

Balance the home where you have it positioned a little above center, vertically. In this example, you can see a little more of the driveway and front yard than the sky. What's more important, the front of the house leading to the street or the sky behind it?

Additionally, by placing the home slightly above vertical center, it does not appear to be falling out of the picture and is

more pleasing to the eye from a compositional point of view. Don't shoot the house when it is in the shade. Here the bright sky behind takes center stage and makes the house really difficult to see. The owner isn't selling the sky. They are selling a house and it is the house that must command all of the attention.

If the home you have staged is open and airy, try to feature that in your shots. People buy homes that look spacious to them. Keep the decorating simple and understated.

If the home has extra high walls, and especially if they feature assets like additional windows, get as low as you can get to take the shot. There's nothing wrong with lying on your stomach to get an upward trending shot of the room. Spaciousness isn't just at eye level. Spaciousness goes out and it also goes up. Try to capture that in your after shots especially for a fantastic look.

If you can get a shot from the top of the stairs, this is a great way to create a feeling of spaciousness even though the actual space may be quite small.

Avoid taking pictures that are too dark. A daytime shot of this home would be far more effective. The angle should also be adjusted to feature the entry of the home, not necessarily the garage. This would also help eliminate a tree from taking center stage as seen here.

High contrast can be used quite effectively for attracting attention. When competing with other homes, you need to present photos that grab the attention as much as possible.

Even though I adjusted the light in this picture quite a bit for reproduction, it is still very dark. You don't want people to have to struggle to see the various elements in the room. So when you're shooting a room with very little contrast or "tone-on-tone" (decorated in all one color), you have to be especially careful that you get enough contrast so it will reproduce well.

If the home includes some really special element (like this fountain) that separates it from all others, be sure to feature it. Make your pictures memorable.

This home, situated on a beautiful canal, came with a fabulous headline which read,

"LIVE ON THE WATER . . . OR WISH YOU DID. WHICH WILL IT BE?"

Don't rely solely on the pictures to sell your services. Create headlines that sizzle and sparkle and conjure up all sorts of hidden wishes and dreams. It's not just about buying or selling a house – it's about buying or selling a dream.

Your pictures should conjure up memories, forgotten fantasies and wishes, the unattainable made possible. When your services help a buyer gain an emotional connection with the home, you've done your job beautifully.

Oftentimes track homes or divisions have names that captivate the heart, such as Seabridge, Renaissance, Indian Oaks, Arboreta. Include the descriptive names of the developer. This helps you romance the home and how you managed it for your client. This is far better than referring to the home as 124 Dirtpile Road. Just kidding, but you get the point, right?

Turn all the lights on when you shoot inside, even if it is still day time. The sparkle and shadows that lights will create against the ceiling and walls will add depth to your pictures and give the room a warmer feeling.

Don't let the trees grab all the attention. Look for angles that diminish this type of feeling pictured here. Better to try and get two sides of the house than to make the trees the focal point – better yet, get the seller to trim them or remove them altogether.

Clean a home and de-cluttering it works very well every time. When staging a home and addressing the outside, look for ways to unify the landscaping and de-emphasize anything that blocks view of the house. Yards can be changed, but the house needs to be the focus.

Shooting straight on may get the whole front of the house in the shot, but in this case all one seems to notice is the large tree right in the front looking a bit out of place and in the way. By altering the angle you can keep this from happening to your pictures. By moving more to the left, the tree would not be planted right in the middle of the shot, and you'd still be able to see the garage. It just would be more pleasing to the eye compositionally if the shot were taken at an angle.

This picture was shot at sunset by the agent, which is nice if the picture is shown in color. But it was much darker than I'm showing here and so far away, one finds it extremely difficult to see much of anything. I understand this is a ranch-style

home, but it doesn't do that much good if you can't see it and have to strain at that. Don't make people take extra effort to view your pictures.

When you can, try to include two sides of the house in your picture. This creates more interest and depth and makes the home look much larger than it might be. It's usually pretty obvious as to which of the two sides of the house gives you the best photo when shot together with the front.

Here is a typical empty room. The stager captured one wall and part of another one and the lighting fixture. Capturing the lighting fixture is important so that when you see it again in the after shot, you know immediately that it is the same room.

Next is a kitchen with an ugly bare spot where a refrigerator would normally be placed. But because the stager or seller wasn't going to bring in a refrigerator while the house was showing, the stager treated the area cleverly to minimize the negative effect.

Before

After

By showing pictures
like these two, you
teach the seller to become a problem solver.

Demonstrate how
furniture from
one room can be
better utilized in
another room or
in a different

place in the same room to give a professional arrangement. In the before shot, there was no rhyme or reason for why the buffet was placed where it was. Now it looks fabulous and serves a purpose.

I'm showing you pictures from portfolios of some of my students because I want you to see that anyone, and I do mean anyone, can learn to give good advice. It takes more knowledge to be a home stager, but as you can see, ordinary people just like you have started their own businesses from taking my courses and have pulled together the images to go into their own portfolios and on their websites. You can still get good pictures to use to promote your listing services, but you'll need to rely on the sellers you serve to follow directions and bring it about.

Bathrooms are quite easy to do unless toilets, vanities or shower/tubs need to be replaced. But when the bath is in excellent condition, all that is needed is a personal touch – some accessories placed in the right places. Quite easy.

See how much more appealing the bath is now. More elaborate baths will give greater opportunities to create a spa-like atmosphere, but even a tiny bathroom can be enhanced with little effort.

Watch out when you've got shutters or drapes that are open in the background as you'll get a picture that looks like this if you don't adjust your camera settings. This is called backlighting and the camera sets the exposure from the light coming in and makes everything else photograph too dark.

Unless you know how to change your camera settings, close the shutters or drapes before taking your pictures so that the furnishings in the foreground can be seen. Even partially closed blinds are better than blinds that are left fully open. See how dark the room is? The camera picked up the light coming in from the shutters and darkened everything in the foreground.

Watch out for items in the room, especially in the foreground that can ruin a picture. Here the left over lunch items were accidentally left on the counter making the picture pretty useless for a portfolio. On the next page is a better picture for one's portfolio.

This was a little girl's bedroom before the stager worked on the room. Pretty cluttered, right?

Now here is the after shot, but since the seller wouldn't let the stager remove the little shelf (Elise), and it is way out of scale and proportion for the wall, this would be an excellent time to manipulate the picture later and remove the shelf totally.

Now let's see what has been done to improve the picture for use in a portfolio. First I removed the shelf unit with the girl's name (Elise). I also removed the electrical outlet near the floor by the desk (left side). I also removed part of the date so as not to date the picture. These are just simple adjustments you can make yourself to your digital images in a photo editing program.

It's better to remove something from the photo that jumps out at you when it is all wrong than to leave it in. I'm no photo specialist, but I've learned how to use some of the simple tools in my software to accomplish what needs to be done. You can do the same thing. It just takes a little practice and if you need help, there should be plenty of knowledgeable people around you to help you.

Look for angles that really enhance the design elements of what you've been able to achieve. Angular shots show depth better than shots that are taken straight on. They are also more interesting to look at.

Here the shades look lovely rolled half way up but they don't do much for the ability to get a good shot that is not washed in too much light. Try them all the way down as a precaution and then experiment with them rolled up and see what the end results are before leaving the room.

Look for ways to show two walls at the same time. Here we have a nice shot of the dining room table staged for an open house, and it sets off the buffet in the background making it a very nice looking space.

See the spaciousness in this shot of the same home.
I hope you're getting the idea. Each room will dictate where you need to stand to get the best picture when you're all done.

Some will be easier than others.

Look for ways to get close ups and distance shots. If you're working in an open area such as this, where the kitchen, dining room and family room are not separated by walls, try to capture that feeling in your work. These are the kinds of pictures that are ideal for anyone's portfolio.

Of course, any time you have a room that feels chaotic and is extremely cluttered, it's pretty easy to make instant improvements by rearranging the furniture and accessories. This costs the seller nothing and only requires your time to figure out a better arrangement and advise them accordingly.

Any time your seller can see that they've made a significant improvement to a room, they are gaining respect for you and your talents and moving closer to a great referral source for you and a more profitable sale for themselves.

This stager did a magnificent job in rearranging this room. By placing the sofa on an angle and moving the TV, by filling up the shelves with more accessories and changing out the scale and proportions, the room has taken on a real charm and even though there is more in the room now than before, it appears orderly and organized. Actually when advising a seller, have them edit a room like this even more, even if they are still living in the home. As I've stated repeatedly, when it comes to staging, <u>less is generally more</u>.

By carefully shooting your rooms before you give any advice to the seller and shooting them again after the staging has been completed, it won't take you long to build enough pictures for a very impressive portfolio.

Looking Over the Shoulders of a Talented Professional Stager Specializing in Affluent Homes

It is true that all stagers are not alike. They do not have the same backgrounds, nor do they have the same training, nor the same natural talent. For this reason, looking at their professional portfolios will help determine whether their style of staging is suitable to your seller's home. But there are some gems out there that deserve special recognition.

Debbie Muccillo took my Gold Staging Course a few years ago and has blossomed into one of the best stagers in the country. Out of over 15,000+ students, who have flowed through my training programs, Debbie excels among the top 1%. For this reason I decided to feature some of her work right here so you'll see first hand the benefits a highly trained stager can bring to a seller and to virtually any agent.

I've proudly watched her grow and develop her talents. She has improved from year to year. Her work is creative and always suitable for the style of the home and the client's budget. Debbie manages her own inventory and obviously can professionally stage any style home.

Debbie's company is called **Interiors Within Reach** and she is located in Laguna Beach. Any agent listing homes located in Orange County is encouraged to contact Debbie through her website at http://www.interiorswithinreach.com. Be sure to mention you read about her in this manual. It is rare that I endorse the work of a student, but I have no qualms about recommending Debbie. I'm sure you'll agree with that assessment after seeing some of her work in the next few pages.

Before Staging

After Staging

Before Staging

After Staging

Before Staging

After Staging

Before Staging

After Staging

Before Staging

After Staging

Before Staging

After Staging

Chapter 29
Creating an Outstanding Staging Portfolio

Reasons for Creating a Staging Portfolio

So why should you create a staging portfolio? Fair question. The short and simple answer is so that you can gain an edge over other agents who don't offer staging consultations or advice. So that you can help the seller with practical, proven advice that will give them the best shot at selling their home for maximum profit in the shortest period of time.

You've got to understand that selling real estate is as much a visual process as it is facts and figures. No one falls in love with a home unless they are visually touched. Facts and figures, location and pricing reach their intellectual minds; but it is the visual impact of seeing a house's potential that reaches the emotional side and triggers or prompts the buyer to say, "This is the home I want to buy."

Therefore it stands to reason that having great visuals of the seller's property plays a key role in getting the property to sell. As they say, "A picture is worth a thousand words." But what kind of picture will you and the seller be creating? In this guide I've attempted to give you the basics of staging a home, some of the more crucial tactics and strategies. In the end, the worth of your advice and how it plays out will be judged by pictures (and perhaps some video) – but mainly by your pictures.

Future sellers will want to see what kind of difference you have been able to make for others. You cannot and should not try to <u>tell</u> them when you can so easily <u>show</u> them with a staging portfolio. Naturally your portfolio will be filled with all the things you already use to convince a seller that you are the right agent for them.

It's amazing how many agents try to get by on a business card and a brochure – or on sheer reputation. Don't make that mistake. The benefits of having and preparing a top notch portfolio, full of pictures and other material I will outline for you here can make all the difference for you and for them. If they don't understand how much you will benefit them in their quest, they will likely pass you by for someone else who convinces them that they are the right agent.

Most people are visual learners so you need to give them great visuals to look at to support what you are saying and claiming.

Understanding Your Strengths

In my book titled <u>Staging Portfolio Secrets</u> I include advanced strategies for dissecting you and your unique background and pulling out all of the powerful traits and accomplishments that make you special, outstanding and accomplished which will impress anyone. It is such an in-depth discussion I cannot include it here.

But suffice to say, knowing who you are and what assets you bring to the table will jump start and dramatically improve any one's portfolio or list of accomplishments.

If you don't understand all the nuances and facets of your personality and accomplishments, how can you expect anyone else to appreciate them? So a great portfolio starts with identifying your assets and setting them forth.

Before and After Pictures

A great portfolio will also include a host of up-to-date before and after pictures that show the huge improvements staging efforts have made for others. If you have a plethora of staged homes in your portfolio you will rarely have to convince anyone of the benefits of staging a home. The only questions will be what to do, how to do it and who is to do it.

You may have other agents in your office who have staging pictures you can borrow temporarily until you get your own. Offer to let them use yours down the road in exchange. By adding a nice selection of staging photos you will encourage sellers to actively pursue the tactics of professional stagers in one way or another. Even a little helps a lot.

Articles, News Clips and Statistics

Earlier in this book I listed some powerful statistics you should communicate to a seller. Statistics will impact them intellectually. If you have a seller with a strong analytic mind, you'll gain great ground by having some statistics to toss out to them. Take each statistic and print it up in large type on a page of its own. Or put them in a bulleted list for the seller to see as you are explaining the statistic to them. Remember, people remember better when they see something in writing as they listen to you speak.

Check your local newspaper every day looking for articles about staging or other subjects that help to sell homes in your area. By adding articles to your portfolio it has the effect of adding a third party endorsement to your representation. Sellers will appreciate that you are on top of what's happening in the local real estate market and on the look-out for any strategy that will help them sell their house.

List of Check Lists

Do not include a full checklist within the portfolio. No seller should obtain the ability to see the checklist I've made available for you to use until or unless you ARE the listing agent.

Instead pull out the checklist booklet and show them that you have one and that you will be happy to work with them to take full advantage of its power once you are their listing agent. But do not give them a copy of it or allow them to peruse it at their leisure.

However, I do suggest that you prepare a document to include in your portfolio that <u>lists</u> the checklist booklet (<u>Home Staging for Yourself</u>) as one of the resources you will make available to them after they hire you. Any additional checklists or handouts that you will make available should also be identified on this page. This page will become a permanent part of your portfolio.

Feature Sheets You'll Give the Seller

Naturally you'll be making up some sell sheets for the seller to have available at Open House events and to mail out or give out. But another good handout to make available after you are the listing agent is a Features Sheet which itemizes the assets of the home AND the community. Most agents don't do this but it can be a great selling tool for you to utilize.

Awards, Certificates, Designations

Most of us have been taught to refrain from speaking about our accomplishments. While it is mandatory that you let prospects know what sets you apart from the competition, it can be a tricky road to travel. None of us want anyone to be thought of as braggarts.

By including documents in your portfolio that highlight past awards, certificates, designations, articles written about you, interviews by the press and so forth in your portfolio, it has a much different, totally positive outcome. Sellers will appreciate knowing about your achievements if they are interested in a quiet, relaxed understated fashion. So don't hesitate to include these all important documents. Tell the seller you are merely helping them get to know you better.

Making More Than One Portfolio

Common sense tells you that it is important to create more than one portfolio just in case one gets lost, stolen or destroyed. You want to have the assurance that you always have one at your disposal. I advocate that you make up at least five portfolios. If you don't want them to be identical, you might figure out a certain portfolio to use in specific circumstances while having a different one for other circumstances. But in every case, have at least one back-up portfolio for each type you create.

For instance, say you connected with a seller because you were recommended by a home stager. Naturally the seller already has someone to stage the home and you won't want to step on the stager's toes. So a portfolio that doesn't mention your free staging consultation would be appropriate for that seller.

But then let's say you have a seller who has experienced a poor outcome with another agent and has a bad taste for agents in their memory. This type of seller would need to see your staging portfolio so they will see how much greater effort you will put forth on their behalf that the former agent did not.

Take time to visualize all the varying types of sellers you might encounter and determine how many types of portfolios you will need. Then double that so you have plenty of backups.

Mission Statement and Code of Ethics

In an age where there have been so many companies and governmental leaders mislead consumers or downright lie to them, you'll want to be sure to include a document that spells out your mission statement and your personal code of ethics. Don't just say it. Put it in writing.

I recently took my daughter to see a dentist to discuss having veneers put on her upper front teeth. The dentist assured us that he was extremely particular about the quality of the work done by his lab and that even if she was happy with the outcome, if he thought they were not perfect for her he would not let her accept them. He assured us that he would make the lab fix anything that was poorly made until we were completely happy with the results.

Well, it was a very good selling point. But in reality, he kept silent when the first set was placed on my daughter's teeth and it was not until we pointed out a serious problem ourselves that he agreed and was forced to correct the problem.

How much better it would have been for him to take the initiative and tell us what was wrong with the veneers than wait until we complained before he said anything. It left us feeling that his selling proposition was false and that he really couldn't be trusted at the level he promised. As a result he might not get future business from us nor will he get any referrals from us.

Don't make this mistake. If you promise the seller a specific benefit, be sure you deliver exactly what you promise. As a matter of fact, make sure you over-deliver on your promises. Don't assume that because a seller doesn't say anything about broken promises to you that they will keep quiet about it when talking to other people about you. I have never said anything to the dentist about what we have observed, and I don't know if I ever will. But I probably won't be forwarding any other patients his way.

Testimonials

Don't neglect to gather testimonials from sellers after the final outcome has been successful. Naturally you won't want to share any negative testimonials should you get them. But prospects appreciate seeing what other people have experienced under your leadership, so testimonials are an important aspect to a strong portfolio. Keep them to a minimum – say three to five. No one will likely take the time to read them all but probably your top three will be read by every seller who takes the time to peruse your portfolio.

The best testimonials are the ones that refer to your service, your advice and the facts and figures of the final outcome in terms of sold price and the time frame from putting it on the MLS until an offer was accepted. Ask sellers to be specific about what they appreciated in you and about you. Update the list of testimonials regularly because you don't want someone reading a testimonial you got five years ago. A lot can happen in five years. Stay current.

Binding of Your Portfolio

It is important to properly bind your portfolio to withstand transportation and handling. After you leave a portfolio or show it to a seller, there is no telling what can happen to it. Sheets and documents should be placed in protective see-through plastic sleeves. A search at your local office supply store will provide you with a wide variety of binders and suitable plastic protective sleeves for 8.5x11 sheets. If you wish to create a larger scaled portfolio for more impact, visit your local art supply store and take a look at the portfolios that artists and photographers tend to use. There are open binders or ones that have zipper closures but, of course, costs will go up.

You might like to have a more impressive portfolio to show and keep in your possession at all times and a scaled down version to leave with prospective clients.

Marketing With Your Portfolio

Always have one or more portfolios with you. You can keep one on the back seat to remind you to take one into your first meeting with a prospect. Keep another portfolio in the trunk of your car. Keep the rest of your portfolios in your office or at home. With multiple portfolios at your disposal, you can afford to make presentations to multiple sellers all at the same time. The more portfolios you have in circulation at any given time the greater your opportunities are to becoming the listing agent for several sellers at the same time. Nice!

Be sure to cover the one you place on the back seat to protect it from sun damage and so that curious eyes don't get too interested. If you have small children that ride in the back seat, be sure to keep your portfolio well protected so they can't accidentally damage it.

By having a portfolio on your back seat you should remember it when you are taking things out of your vehicle for an appointment. But should you forget, at least it will still be handy to fetch after the meeting gets started.

During the course of showing parts of it to the seller, you'll want to inform them that you will be leaving the portfolio with them overnight (or for a couple of days) so that, at their leisure, they will have plenty of opportunity to go through it and get to know you better. Tell them you want them to feel comfortable with who you are, not just what you can offer them.

Leave the portfolio behind when you are finished with the meeting but make arrangements then as to when you should return to pick it up. Ask them if leaving it overnight or for a couple of nights will give them plenty of time to peruse it.

Don't leave it for more than a couple of nights if you can help it. You want to keep them motivated to make a decision about the agent they will choose. The longer you give them the longer it will take for them to preview the portfolio. It is human nature to put such matters off until the last minute. So keep the time frame short and it will serve you well.

Those agents who have crafted a strong portfolio identifying their strengths, goals, ethics, testimonials and benefits will find themselves with a very strong edge over agents who do not.

Chapter 30
Forms, Agreements and Handouts

This chapter will provide you with some forms, agreements and hand outs that may be useful and save you time. As with all such documents, which you are free to reproduce as you desire, I offer my disclaimer. I am not in the business of dispensing legal advice and do not make any claims as to the benefits or protections any of my forms may actually give. Anyone using them does so of their own choosing and bears all liability and personal responsibility for such use and agrees to hold Barbara Jennings, the publisher and any heirs harmless in any and all matters that might arise as a result of their use.

Memory Retaining Fact Sheet

Date of Visit:

_____

Address of Property

_____
_____
_____

First Impressions

_____
_____
_____
_____
_____
_____
_____
_____
_____
_____
_____
_____
_____

Final Impressions

_____
_____
_____
_____
_____
_____
_____
_____
_____
_____
_____
_____
_____

Family Staging Commitment Agreement

We, _____ family, recognize that we play an integral part in the successful marketing strategies for our home. Staging the home is a crucial part of those strategies. We understand that we are responsible for managing all of the tasks we agree to manage with regard to staging the home and doing by _____. We further understand that we are part of a team and will uphold our end of the agreement to the best of our abilities. Should we anticipate we will be unable to do so, we will communicate instantly with all members of the "team", first and foremost with our agent, so that alternative solutions can be sought which are in our best interests as owners of the property.

_____

Signature of Owner   Date

_____

Signature of Spouse   Date

_____

Signature of Child #1   Date

_____

Signature of Child #2   Date

_____

Signature of Child #3   Date

_____

Signature of Child #4   Date

Stager Recommendation List

To assist you in locating a local professional home stager to prepare your home for sale, please see if any of these recommendations are suitable to you.

STAGER'S NAME   PHONE

_____

EMAIL ADDRESS   WEBSITE

_____

STAGER'S NAME   PHONE

_____

EMAIL ADDRESS   WEBSITE

_____

STAGER'S NAME   PHONE

_____

EMAIL ADDRESS   WEBSITE

_____

STAGER'S NAME   PHONE

_____

EMAIL ADDRESS   WEBSITE

_____

STAGER'S NAME   PHONE

_____

EMAIL ADDRESS   WEBSITE

_____

Box Content List Slip

Packed From
Room_____

- From Location
    - Upstairs
    - Downstairs
    - Attic
    - Basement
    - Garage
    - Front Yard
    - Back Yard
    - Side Yards

Contents of Box:

- _____
- _____
- _____
- _____
- _____

- _____
- _____
- _____
- _____
- _____
- _____
- _____
- _____
- _____
- _____
- _____
- _____
- _____
- _____

Example of Room Feature List

Room_____

Measurements of Room
_____

This Room's Outstanding Features Include:

- _____
- _____
- _____
- _____
- _____
- _____
- _____
- _____
- _____
- _____
- _____
- _____
- _____
- _____
- _____
- _____
- _____
- _____
- _____
- _____
- _____

Neighborhood Lifestyle Sheets

Offer to provide a neighborhood life-style sheet that sellers can make copies of for buyers to pick up.

Features to Include:

- o **Neighborhood Information** - List number and ages of children on the street, include summary of adult occupations and interests, neighborhood associations, neighborhood watch programs.
- o **School and Daycare Information** - Write about quality of schools. Get information from school district. If they have brochures, pick up some copies to leave out. List public and private schools: preschool, elementary, middle and high school. List community colleges and 4-year colleges and universities. Include information on school bus pickups.
- o **Babysitters** - Include a list of local babysitters if you have them.
- o **Recreational Information** - Include list of parks, sports clubs, recreational clubs, community playhouse theaters, movie theaters, museums, libraries.
- o **Local Retailers** - List your favorite stores in the area: grocery stores, department stores, dry cleaners, shoe repairs, video stores, hairdressers, restaurants (fast food and sit-down), children's' stores.
- o **Access to Freeways**. State the directions to and average time of travel to freeways.
- o **Utilities** - List contact information for electricity, gas, water and trash and give the average costs for the home.
- o **Personal Letter** - Include a description of living there and how the town or city has changed and improved. Emphasize the quietness, any favorable weather assets, length of time neighbors have lived

there, special opportunities not available elsewhere and so forth. Share some of your best memories living in the home.

Carpet Care and Stain Removal Guide

Day to Day Care
1. Vacuum frequently
2. Clean spills promptly
3. Have periodic professional carpet cleaning. (Brite-World)

Appearance
1. Sprouting - Shoe nails, pet claws, or defective cleaning equipment can pull tufts above the level of the rest of the carpet. Trim sprouts with a sharp pair of scissors.
2. Shedding - Short broken fibers can become trapped in the yarn during the yarn making process. After their carpet is installed, these short, unattached fibers show up on the surface of the carpet as fuzz. Some shedding is normal for the high quality spun yarn used in a fine carpet. A few weeks of vacuuming will eliminate the condition.
3. Shading - Heavy traffic sometimes cause tufts to lie in opposite directions. The tufts that remain upright appear darker than those lying on their side. A thorough vacuuming or combing the pile with a pile rake will lift compressed tufts and reduce shading.
4. Mildew - Gulistan carpet is designed to reduce mildew. However, when humidity is high or the carpet is continually moist, your carpet could develop mildew. If mildew should appear, first eliminate the moisture problem, then have a cleaning professional treat the carpet with fungicide.
5. Pilling - Pills are small, fuzzy balls that stick to the carpet surface. They are caused by strong, unbroken fibers clinging to weak fibers broken by defective or improper cleaning equipment. Gulistan carpets should not pill after the first few weeks. If pilling continues, the fibers should be carefully trimmed and all cleaning equipment inspected for worn or broken rollers, beater bars and brushes. Pets may also cause pills in the carpet.

6. Furniture Dents - The weight of heavy furniture will crush the pile underneath and cause an indentation. Holding a steam iron over (never against) the indented area will help restore the pile. If possible, you should rearrange your furniture periodically to reduce permanent damage indentations.

Preventing Issues
1. Dirt isn't just dirty. It can actually harm your carpet. If allowed to accumulate, small particles will wear individual fibers, weakening the carpet.
2. Place walk-off mats at all outside entrances, use runners in high-traffic areas, and rearrange furniture periodically to reduce wear and dirt. The most important preventative measure you can take is proper vacuuming. Vacuum your carpet at least once or twice weekly, depending on the amount of traffic.
3. A vacuum cleaner with a motor driven brush attachment will work better than one that uses suction only. Follow your machine's directions for carpet height adjustment. Do not vacuum sticky or greasy stains.

Spills and Stains
1. Your carpet gets rough treatment everyday. Sooner or later, accidents will happen. Fortunately, your Gulistan carpet features the latest stain-resistant fibers. So cleaning is easier than ever before.
2. As soon as you discover a spill, follow theses steps. A. Remove as much of the spill as possible. Scrape up the solid material with a putty knife or other flat, blunt tool, moving from the outside of the spill to the center. Blot wet spots. B. Refer to the Stain Removal Procedures for cleaning instructions. C. Let the carpet dry completely; then brush the pile to restore texture. D. Repeat procedure if necessary. E. Consult a professional carpet cleaner if the stain persists. Tell the cleaner the type of stain, type of carpet fiber, color of carpet, style of carpet (cut pile, cut and loop pile, loop pile), carpet age, general condition, and cleaning method already used.

Stain Cleaning Methods (see explanation of each method below the list)

Acid Toilet Bowl Cleaner E
Acne Medication E
Alkaline Drain Cleaner E
Asphalt D
Beer A
Beet Juice B
Bleach E
Blood A
Candle Wax I
Carbon Black (soot) E
Carbonated Cola (dark) A
Carbonated Fruit Flavored Soda A
Ketchup A
Chocolate D
Coffee H
Cooking Oil/Soil D
Cough Syrup (FD & C colors) A
Cranberry Juice H
Crayon D
Dimethylsulfoxide E
Dirty Motor Oil D
Drink Mix A
Egg A
Feces C
Furniture Polish E
Furniture Stain D
Gelatin A
Grape Juice B then H
Grease D
Hair Dye E
Ice Cream D

Ink (water soluble) A
Ink (ball point) D
Insecticide E
Iodine A then E
Jam/Jelly (fruit or berry) A
Latex Paint A
Lipstick D
Liqueur A
Liquid Fruit Punch A
Marking Pen (permanent ink) A
Medicine (FD&C colors) A
Mouthwash A
Mustard with Turmeric A
Nail Polish G
Oil Paint D
Orange Juice A
Plant Fertilizer E
Prune Juice B
Red Clay Soil F
Red Wine H
Rouge D
Rust A
Sauce, Spaghetti & Bar-B-Que D
Shoe Dye E
Shoe Polish D
Tea H
Topsoil F
Urine C
Vomit C
Watercolors A

Cleaning Method A

1. Blot excess stain or liquid with paper towels.

2. Wet stain with a minimal amount of water, soak 1 minute, blot with paper towels, and repeat until no stain is evident on towels.

3. Apply small amount of liquid detergent. Massage into stained area with finger tips, blot excess, and repeat until no stain is evident on towels. Rinse with a minimal amount of clear water, and blot.

4. Cover stained area with a layer of paper towels, weight down with a heavy object such as a brick or book. and allow to dry.
5. Repeat Step 4, each time adding a minimal amount of water; until blotter no longer picks up any stain.
6. Brush up pile of carpet and allow to dry thoroughly. (Turmeric will fade under strong light)

Cleaning Method B
1. Blot excess stain or liquid with paper towels.
2. Wet stain with a minimal amount of water, soak 1 minute, blot with paper towels, and repeat until no stain is evident on towels.
3. Apply first 3% hydrogen peroxide then ammonia to stained area. Blot, rinse with clear water; and blot up excess with paper towels.
4. Apply small amount of liquid detergent to stained area. Massage in with fingertips, blot excess, and repeat until no stain is evident on towels. Rinse with a minimal amount of clear water, and blot.
5. Cover stained area with a layer of paper towels, weight down with a heavy object such as a brick or book, and allow to dry.
6. Repeat step 5, each time adding a minimal amount of clear water, until blotter no longer shows any stain.
7. Brush up pile of carpet and allow to dry thoroughly.

Cleaning Method C
1. Blot excess stain or liquid with paper towels.
2. Vacuum up particulate. Soften stain with a small amount of dry-cleaning solvent, blot with paper towels, and repeat until no stain shows on blotter.
3. Apply small amount of liquid detergent. Massage into stained area with fingertips, blot excess, and repeat until no stain is evident on towels. Rinse with a minimal amount of clear water and blot.

4. Cover stained area with a layer of paper towels, weight down with a heavy object such as a brick or book, and allow to dry.
5. Repeat step 4, each time adding a minimal amount of clear water, until blotter no longer shows any stain.
6. Brush up pile and allow to dry thoroughly.

Cleaning Method D
1. Blot excess stain or liquid with paper towels.
2. Wet stain with a small amount of alcohol or dry cleaning solvent, blot dry immediately, and repeat until no stain shows on blotter.
3. Apply small amount of liquid detergent. Massage into stained area with fingertips, blot excess, and repeat until no stain in evident on towels. Rinse with a minimal amount of clear water and blot.
4. Cover stained area with a layer of paper towels, weight down with a heavy object such as a brick or book, and allow to dry.
5. Repeat Step 4, each time adding a minimal amount of clear water, until blotter no longer shows any stain.
6. Brush up pile of carpet and allow to dry thoroughly.

Cleaning Method E
1. Blot to remove excess stain or liquid with paper towels.
2. Rinse stain with a minimal amount of clear water, and blot dry with paper towels.
3. Have damaged areas replaced (plugged) by a professional carpet installer.

Cleaning Method F
1. Allow residue to dry.
2. Vacuum up particulate.
3. Wet stain with a minimal amount of water, soak 1 minute, blot with paper towels, and repeat until no stain is evident on towels.
4. Apply small amount of liquid detergent. Massage into stained area with fingertips, blot excess, and repeat until no

stain is evident on towels. Rinse with a minimal amount of clear water, and blot.

5. Cover stained area with a layer of paper towels, weight down with a heavy object such as a brick or book, and allow to dry.

6. Repeat Step 5, each time adding a minimal amount of clear water, until blotter no longer shows any stain.

7. Brush up pile of carpet and allow to dry thoroughly.

Cleaning Method G

1. Blot excess to remove stain or liquid.

2. Apply a small amount of nail polish remover, blot immediately and repeat until no stain shows on blotter.

3. Apply small amount of liquid detergent, massage into stained area with fingertips, blot excess, and repeat until no stain is evident on towels. Rinse with a minimal amount of clear water, and blot.

4. Cover stained area with a layer of paper towels, weight down with a heavy object such as a brick or book, and allow to dry.

5. Repeat Step 4, each time adding a minimal amount of clear water, until blotter no longer shows any stain.

6. Brush up pile of carpet and allow to dry thoroughly.

Cleaning Method H

1. Blot to remove excess stain or liquid.

2. Wet stained area with a minimal amount of club soda or tonic water, blot with paper towels, and repeat wetting and blotting until no stain is evident on towels.

3. Rinse with minimal clear water.

4. Apply small amount of liquid detergent. Massage into stained area with fingertips, blot excess, and repeat until no stain is evident on towels. Rinse with a minimal amount of clear water, and blot.

5. Apply 3% hydrogen peroxide. Let stand 4 hours, blot, and repeat procedure. Allow to stand 24 hours, blot, then allow to air dry for 48 hours. If stain is still evident, repeat procedure until stain is no longer visible. Rinse with clear water and

blot dry.

6. Brush up pile of carpet and allow to dry thoroughly.

Cleaning Method I

1. Allow wax to harden.
2. Freeze with ice and chip off excess.
3. Wet stain with small amount of dry cleaning solvent. Blot immediately with paper towels. Repeat until no stain is evident on blotter.
4. Apply small amount of liquid detergent. Massage into stained area with fingertips, blot excess, and repeat until no stain is evident on towels. Rinse with a minimal amount of clear water, and blot.
5. Cover stained area with a layer of paper towels, weight down with a heavy object such as a brick or book, and allow to ry.
6. Repeat Step 5, each time adding a minimal amount of clear water, until blotter no longer picks up any stain.
7. Brush up pile of carpet and allow to dry thoroughly.

Garage Sale Tips for Sellers

- Choose a weekend date for most traffic.
- Thoroughly clean all items for sale.
- Create feeling of outdoor "fair", not a garage sale.
- Tie colorful balloons to a tree, mailbox or back of chairs.
- Play light energetic music.
- Dress all helpers in the same color t-shirts or matching hats or aprons.
- Be early in your preparations. Shoppers tend to ignore the start times. Be sure the garage sale is properly promoted.
- Make and display large, easy to read signs for neighborhood.
- Avoid hand lettered signs.

- Use stencils or a computer to produce signs of quality. Professional looking signs will pull in weekend drivers.
- Place sequence of 3-4 signs on main street in both directions.
- Place additional signs or arrows on side streets.
- Price items based on what you would be willing to pay if you were a buyer.
- Condition is a key factor in pricing. Visit other garage sales to get comparisons and a feeling for what works and what doesn't.
- Leave ample space around all sections for easy browsing.
- Label areas such as: Antiques, House wares, Sporting Goods, Clothing, Toys, Linens, Special Bargains
- Tri-fold clothes for tables; hang on hangers for others.
- Make sure all clothing is labeled for sizes.
- Tie linens together in sets with colorful ribbons.
- Use plastic zip-lock bags to display small items.
- Don't over display tables. If too many items on a table, they will look like junk and sell for less.
- Attach description with dates and pertinent information on antiques and collectibles.
- Watch out for people arriving in a group of two or more. Some may be decoys to distract you while others pocket items without paying for them.
- Put tablecloths on tables; put area rugs or vinyl tarps on cement.
- Use bright colored sale stickers that are easily found.
- Write descriptions and uses out and attach to unusual items.
- Check tables and other areas periodically throughout the day to make sure displays look attractive.
- As inventory at the front of the driveway sells, replace it with other merchandise. This helps attract the "drive by" customers and encourages them to stop and look.

- Place sun umbrella in outdoor table to provide shade when needed.
- Be sure to lock the house. Don't let buyers have opportunity to enter your home or your garage. Block off access and peering eyes to contents in the garage.
- Wear a belted fanny pack around your waist with plenty of change. Do not have a change box on a table.
- Place some folding chairs at the check out tables and other places for you, your helpers or customers to sit.
- To easily test electrical appliances, have a power cord handy. Keep extra marker and price stickers in your fanny pack to replace lost stickers and for end of the day markdowns.
- Prepare snacks and meals in advance for yourself and helpers.
- Place like kinds together: clothes on hangers on rack, dishes and accessories on tables, furniture all in one section.
- Place several calculators around for easy processing.
- Have plenty of bags of various sizes.
- Have plenty of newspapers on hand for wrapping and bagging.
- Have plenty of scotch tape on hand.
- If you don't have much help, have a wrapping table next to the checkout so people can wrap things themselves.
- Be prepared to bargain. Many people assume negotiation is part of the process.
- Remember the goal is to sell out, if possible.
- Remain open, enthusiastic and cheery.
- Consider offering light refreshments, such as lemonade in paper cups.
- Have a "kids only" section.
- Toward end of day, offer extra discounts for multiple purchases.
- Discount all prices by 50% in the last hour. Make a sign to display just for final hour.
- Donate what doesn't sell. Don't keep it.

Open House Check List for Sellers

Exterior

- Pick up and store all toys and lawn tools.
- Pick up and store all pet gear.
- Remove all vehicles from curb and anything else that obstructs view.
- Sweep or hose down driveway and walkways.
- Use leaf blower to give tidy look.
- Clear away debris from pool or hot tub.
- _____
- _____
- _____

Interior

- Empty all wastebaskets.
- Pick up dirty clothes and place in hamper near washing machine.
- Clear all counters, desks, table tops and store papers away.
- Remove any hazards, such as throw rugs, extension cords, small toys.
- Store away all personal items found in bathrooms.
- Clear away all children's toys and straighten beds and room.
- Vacuum, sweep and dust all rooms.
- Sterilize counters, bathtubs, showers, sinks.
- Wipe off all tables and put chairs under tables and desks.
- Arrange fresh floral arrangements in every room.
- Make sure all rugs are cleaned and properly placed.
- Open all shades, curtains, drapes (unless you need to detract from something outside).

- Open some windows to freshen the rooms.
- Turn all lights on in every room.
- Turn soft music on.
- Add fragrance oils in bathrooms and kitchen.
- Add the fragrance of fresh baking.
- _____
- _____

Last Minute Home Enhancement

- Place linens and flower arrangements on table.
- Arrange a book, game or hobby project on the table.
- Turn off all televisions.
- Arrange guest towels in bathrooms and kitchen.
- Put thermostat or air conditioner at a comfortable level.
- Re-check every room for cleanliness and orderliness.
- Leave home and take your pets with you.
- _____
- _____
- _____

Chapter 31
Additional Resources

Free Resources

I have a number of free resources that might be of interest to you. More details are available at my website, but here is a quick run-down on them.

Free Monthly Decorating Newsletters

Twice a month I send out free decorating newsletters to anyone upon request. Send your request to twodovelane@gmail.com and we'll gladly add your email to our database. We never rent, sell or give away anyone's email address for any reason, so you can sign up knowing you are protected from spam of any kind.

Free Decorating Tips Pages

I also have hundreds of free decorating tips on a wide assortment of subjects. To see an easy list of all of these tips and the links to all of those pages, please visit: http://www.decorate-redecorate.com/master-sitemap.html

Certification

Home Staging Certification

The certification for home stagers offered by the Academy of Staging and Redesign is first rate. There is enormous respect for this designation (CSS – Certified Staging Specialist) because a stager must pass an exam and submit a portfolio of their work before qualifying to receive it. While it is a bit time consuming to go through the process, it is well worth the effort. Certification fees are part of any course but if it is sought independently, there is a fee you must pay.

Certification not only affirms that a candidate has the knowledge and talent to be a professional stager it can be effectively used in marketing efforts to gain an edge over those who have not attained comparable designations based on talent and knowledge. For more information, please read the requirements here: http://www.decorate-redecorate.com/certified-redesigner.html

Agent Certification

Consider qualifying for our new designation just for agents: Certified Real Estate Home Staging Advisor (CREHSA) designation. You must pass an exam (which should be easy if you read this entire book), pay a nominal fee and show proof of a current real estate license. I will send you a certificate sanctioned by the Academy indicating that you have passed the exam and are deemed qualified to offer quality free home staging advice. See my website for details.

Chapter 32
Closing Thoughts

Congratulations!

If you got all the way to the end of this book, you are to be congratulated as someone genuinely wanting to improve your career. Many people will start but not all will finish. We are all created equal – but we will not finish as equals.

Many people talk a big game but lack the follow thru skills necessary to achieve what they say they want. Adding home staging, as it has merits for your seller, takes time and effort on your part. It will not happen and you and your seller will not derive benefits from the process without work and commitment.

Just last week I got an email from a gal who had her real estate license and had been an agent for some time. She has grown a thriving home staging business over the past decade and shared a wonderful story with me. I pass it along to you just in case you are considering altering your career to become a professional stager in addition to or separate from being an agent.

"While I still hold a California real estate license, I have not been active since I started staging, other than for my own house. Early on, I was able to form a core of the top producing agents and I have treated them very well. And most of them have stayed with me for the last 14 years and referred me to many others. Targeting those agents from the very beginning is the key to this business I believe. They do the bulk of the business. What is it? Ten percent of the agents do 90% of the business? Those agents are my main clients. So we try and keep things as simple as we can for them.

"We get to know their style, their level of involvement, their likes and dislikes. In most cases, if you keep those agents happy, they will run interference for you with the sellers and back up what you do. It makes life much easier.

"Last summer we threw a huge party for them launching our website at a Tesla Motors showroom that was completely staged! Great fun, lots of wine and we were able to get our message across.

"The beauty of our website is that each of our staged homes is on our website that links to the agent's website. This gives them additional marketing support. The business has grown so quickly that it has been difficult to keep up.

"We are currently set up with the systems and crew to stage 4 houses per day. My crew is amazing and have been with me 6 years on average. I sometimes think staging is interior design on steroids! . . . Each and every project is a unique project. We mix and match and the inventory has been chosen for that purpose.

"We have to be able to address every form of architecture in this area. I have done everything from an original Victorian to a converted loft that was once a train station.

"In the beginning, I had absolutely no working capital. I staged the first house with furniture from my own house! And I took the money from that and bought some more furniture. Right now I have 4 warehouses totaling 8600 square feet. We have 2 box trucks and 2 vans. And now once again we are expanding.

"We are starting to do the project management and we are having a terrific response. Our latest project is the house _____ which is on our website. This sold in two days with multiple offers.

"We did everything to this house--new hardwood floors for the entire first floor, totally new kitchen including cabinets, 3 new bathrooms, all new light fixtures and plumbing fixtures, new carpet downstairs, new hardware and doors throughout, a new front door, painting inside and out, new tile in the kitchen and entry--all completed in less than 2 months and for under 70k. My project manager has such a gift in finding materials that look outrageously expensive for very low prices. He did a terrific job and so right now we are "launching" the new division.

". . . I can never complain about having work however. I have been very blessed." - Christine Cooper, CSS

The Opportunities Are There

When times are tough I'm often asked if there really and truly is money to be made in home staging. You may still wonder if staging advice will really benefit you. I can only tell you that smart agents add it to their strategies. Let's face it. It's all common sense anyway. But you'd be amazed at how many people are content to "just get by" doing things the same old fashioned way, never seeking to improve their knowledge or skill.

Staging works! Just looking at before and after pictures you inherently know it works. People buy because they become emotionally impacted by a residence. How can they become emotionally attached to a bare home? How can they become emotionally attached to a messy home, or a smelly home or a dirty home? Pricing is important, but it's not the only important thing.

Now you have the basic knowledge of what home staging is all about. Hopefully you feel confident to give good, effective advice to your clients. That's what this book is all about.

I don't expect you to offer staging services yourself, unless you want to and are legally able to do so. Please do not take any path that would put you in legal jeopardy with your State's requirements for your real estate license. That would be terribly unwise.

If you want to profit from staging services, <u>make sure you are entitled to do so first</u>. If you plan on charging for your advice or services, I strongly urge you to take a course so that you are properly prepared to conduct a professional business. Check with your broker and State to make sure you are not violating any legal requirement that affects your license.

I have enjoyed this journey with you and I wish you all the best – either as an agent offering free advice or as a full service home stager.

Go for it.

God bless you.

Warm regards,
Barbara Jennings, Author/Director
The Academy of Staging and Redesign
Decorate-Redecorate.com

Contact the Author
Academy of Staging and Redesign
Decorate-Redecorate.Com
Box 2632, Costa Mesa, CA 92628-2632
twodovelane@gmail.com

OTHER BOOKS BY THE AUTHOR

INSPIRATIONAL
Echoes in Eternity

HOME STAGING BUSINESS
Home Staging for Profit (Start a Staging Business)
Staging Portfolio Secrets
Staging Luxurious Homes
Getting Paid: Financial Strategies for Home Stagers
Home Staging in Tough Times
Home Staging for Yourself
A Real Estate Agent's Guide . . . to Offering Free Advice

INTERIOR RE-DESIGN AND CORPORATE ART
Rearrange It! How to Start and Grow a Redesign Business
Arrange Your Stuff (Advanced Arrangement Training)
Advanced Redesign
Wall Groupings: How to Arrange Your Art and Photos
Dos and Don'ts in Staging and Redesign
Pro Art Consulting

EBOOKS (available from the Author)
Décor Secrets Revealed   Advanced Redesign
Home Staging for Profit   Great Parties–Great Homes
Rearrange It!   Pro Art Consulting

KINDLE eBooks (available from Amazon)
40 Bad Habits You Must Avoid
13 Ways to Improve Your Relationships
Middle School Survival Guide

WHERE TO PURCHASE
Books by the author are available at Amazon.Com or from her website
(http://decorate-redecorate.com).

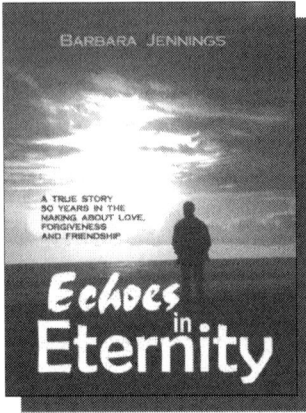

A POWERFUL TRUE STORY

My personal story and that of my best friend and business partner, an incredible human being, Dave Fahs. It is a true story of our 51-year journey together - two obscure people living relatively obscure lives, but how we coped with truly unordinary circumstances which ultimately drew us closer to each other and closer to God.

180 pages, soft cover
Proceeds go to charities fighting cancer
2017 Edition now published
Available at Amazon.Com

UNSOLICITED REVIEWS OF THE BOOK:

"Most of the time when i read it is to put me to sleep, which generally occurs about 3 lines into a paragraph. In Barbara Jennings book, *Echos In Eternity*, it was an entirely different story. From the moment i picked it up i was riveted. Every time i read the book it would wake me up! I would be so engaged in the book that a chapter would fly by and i would have to force myself to put it down because i had to get some sleep! I would look forward to reading it during the day, and i couldn't wait to get to it! It was one of the best books i have read in years and i want more from this author! It was such a touching, heart-warming and inspiring story. Everyone who has ever had someone close to them will be impacted by this evocative adventure in deep relationship. I wish everyone would to themselves and the ones they love a huge favor by reading this book! You would be so grateful you did as it will move you to appreciate those closest to you!" *Grant Godfrey*

"I found this book captivating from beginning to end! From the author's early life in Japan as the daughter of American missionaries to her seeming endless quest for love, purpose and acceptance; there was a constant ribbon winding through every victory and each defeat, of God's provision, love and grace. No matter what circumstances life thrust upon her, she was always able to find that ribbon and hold to it and see God in every horizon! It was a remarkable story of love and loyalty, despite intriguing odds, unique circumstances and challenging attitudes and relationships. A story of personal strength, filled with grace, love and courage! It was, in my opinion, a very good read!" *James Irby*

ANNOUNCING NEW ARTISTIC PRODUCTS AT TWODOVELANE.COM

We are pleased to announce some new fine art available that is very unique and personalized. You can now *submit a photo of your choice via email* and we'll turn it into a personalized *PhotoFineArt original* for you.

Photos can be of you, a spouse, relative, child, friend – even your pet. What fun to see your favorite photo transformed into fine art suitable for framing and uniquely designed just for you.

For plenty of <u>full color</u> examples and to commission online, please visit **TwoDoveLane.Com**. We call this PhotoFineArt.

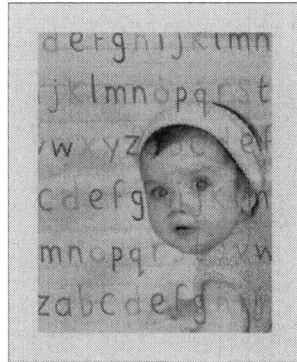

You can see a wide variety of work we've already done and would be very pleased to create something for you. All PhotoFineArt comes 8x10 on acid free paper with an 11x14 white mat, a backing board and a clear protective sleeve. Framing is left to buyer. Images shipped flat.

10694687R00136

Printed in Great Britain
by Amazon